# 'You'll Never Die, John A.!'

# 'You'll Never Die, John A.!'

EDWIN C. GUILLET

1967
Macmillan of Canada
Toronto

Permission to quote from the following copyrighted
material is gratefully acknowledged:
The passages from *John A. Macdonald, The Young
Politician* and *John A. Macdonald, The Old Chieftain*
by D. G. Creighton are reprinted by permission of the
author. Those from *Reminiscences, Political and
Personal* by Sir John Willison are reprinted by
permission of the Canadian publishers, McClelland
and Stewart Limited.

Printed in Canada

*To the memory of my uncle, George Guillet of Cobourg, Member of Parliament for West Northumberland, returned in the general elections of 1882, 1887, and 1896 and in by-elections in 1881, 1885, and 1892, devoted colleague of Sir John A. Macdonald*

# Contents

# List of Illustrations

# Preface

Canada's Centennial Year provides an appropriate occasion for a fresh look at the life and times of Sir John Macdonald, who was known familiarly and affectionately throughout his political career as 'John A.'.

The title is the inspired shout of a supporter at a Toronto election meeting in 1884. It could easily have been drowned out in the enthusiasm and applause with which he was being greeted, but it came at a silent moment just as the leader was telling his followers, a little wistfully, that he had not been in the best of health. Everyone heard it, and John A. commented upon it with that extempore humour he could always muster to suit an occasion.

The materials presented in this book could not have been assembled on short order. Some twenty-five years ago I began collecting colourful items, often from rare sources and unexpected places. The illustrations similarly are largely unknown to the present generation, covering in woodcut, sketch, painting, and photograph Sir John himself, his homes, and the varied activities that filled the life of the successful politician of his day. Never a stuffed shirt, John A. was probably most at home in the House, at election meetings, and at torchlight parades, but he could rise to any occasion and was a part of the liveliness of the times even at a prosaic event like a college convocation. We catch glimpses of him in such diverse places as a pre-Confederation session of Parliament in Quebec City, at a reception in his honour in New Westminster, and at a dance he gave on St. Valentine's Day, 1860.

Text and illustrations are credited to their sources where they appear. I am particularly indebted to Rapid Grip and Batten Ltd. for permission to reproduce Bengough cartoons, to Eleanor Harman, Toronto, to the Public Archives of Canada and the Toronto Public Library for photographs, and to J. Alex. Edmison, Ottawa, Harold Lockwood, Fort William, Harriet Clark, Toronto, and George and Ruth Stanley, Kingston, for making available items from their collections.

*Edwin C. Guillet*

# The Man

Born across the Clyde from Glasgow, Scotland, on January 11, 1815, John A. Macdonald was the eldest son of Hugh Macdonald and Helen Shaw. He came to Canada with his parents in 1820 and spent his youth in Kingston and vicinity. He was educated in the Royal Grammar School, Kingston, called to the bar of Upper Canada in 1836, and was elected to represent Kingston in the Legislative Assembly of Canada in 1844.

In 1854 he was instrumental in forming the coalition of groups which became the Liberal-Conservative Party. He became Attorney General for Canada West the same year, Conservative leader two years later, and Prime Minister in 1857. Deadlock in government resulted in the formation of the 'Great Coalition' which brought about, largely under his leadership and persistence, the confederation of the British North American colonies. Prominent in the Charlottetown, Quebec, and London conferences, where the details of Confederation were worked out, he became the first Prime Minister of the Dominion of Canada in 1867.

In 1872-3 his administration was defeated as a result of the 'Pacific Scandal', and until 1878 his party was in opposition. In that year he led the Conservatives back to power on the 'National Policy' of high protection for Canadian industries, and remained invincible at the polls during the rest of his life. He died on June 6, 1891.

Macdonald ranks highest among Canadian statesmen, and not only because of his unrivalled skill in managing men and softening antagonisms in a most important period of history; his achievements include the safeguarding of law and order under difficulties, the conciliation of French and English and Roman Catholics and Protestants, the union of the provinces, the building of the Canadian Pacific Railway, and the continuance of the British connection. Not without faults, he had among his great qualities vision, tact, patience, and common sense.

John A. Macdonald
Public Archives of Canada

# A Maiden Speech by Johnny

[A brother] died at the age of six – and little Johnny was left to be his mother's only boy. He was noted for having a bright eye, a lively manner, and a head of curly brown hair, which darkened into black as he grew up. His political – or at least his speech-making – career began in Glasgow at the early age of four. One day while some relatives with their children were visiting the house, the little ones were locked up in a room to make a day of it. Among the performances of the day was a maiden speech by Johnny, which certainly made a sensation, but in an unexpected way. The child mounted a table and began to make a speech. What he lacked in language he made up in vehemence of gesticulation; but in the midst of the peroration he was performing with his arms and legs a noise was heard outside, and in the alarm he whirled himself off the table and struck his forehead upon a chair. The incident 'brought down the house' in considerable alarm, and Johnny was found to have a severe cut, a scar which he bore to his dying day.

*Reminiscences of Mrs. John Macpherson, in E. B. Biggar,* Anecdotal Life of Sir John Macdonald *(Montreal, 1891), pp. 13-14.*

I am like those who hear me, a Canadian, heart and soul. I heard the gallant officer who returned thanks for the army and navy say he was. That, I believe, is the feeling that exists in every breast here; and though I have the misfortune, like my friend the deputy adjutant general, to be a Scotchman, still I was caught young, and was brought to this country before I had been very much corrupted.* (Laughter.) Since I was five years old I have been in Canada. My affections, my family are here. All my hopes and my remembrances are Canadian; and not only are my principles and prejudices Canadian, but (what, as a Scotchman, I feel as much as anybody else) my interests are Canadian. (Applause.)

*Address at St. Thomas, 1860.*

---

*John A. was obviously thinking of Dr. Johnson's dictum that much might be done for a Scotchman if he were caught young.

*Memorial Album of Sir John A. Macdonald*

Brunswick Place, near Glasgow

On January 11, 1815, John A. Macdonald was born in the stone tenement house at the left, near the ferry landing across the Clyde from Glasgow.

## In Adolphustown

There was but one board desk in the school house, and that ran round three sides of the room. The teacher's desk was at the vacant end, and a pail of water in the corner was about the only other piece of furniture in this temple of learning, which was presided over by a crabbed old Scotchman known as Old Hughes. Hughes had an adroit method of taking a boy by the collar and giving him a lift off his feet and a whack at the same time. The skill and celerity with which he did this was very interesting to all the boys except the subject of the operation, and Johnny must often have enjoyed the exhibition though he had no love for the chief performer, upon whom he played more than one sly trick. His school mates of this early day described Johnny Macdonald as thin and spindly and pale, and his long lumpy nose gave him such a peculiar appearance that some of the girls called him 'ugly John Macdonald'. (A Scots dominie named Pringle who taught him earlier in Kingston used to say that

'Johnny Macdonald had a heid on him like a mon'.) One of them says he did not show any marked cleverness till later on, when he had got into the study of mathematics. He was not fond of athletics, or of hunting or sport, although he was very nimble and was a fleet runner. He delighted, like most boys in the country, to run barefoot in summer, and often referred in after years in his speeches to this boyish pleasure.

*Biggar,* Anecdotal Life, *p. 24.*

[Sir John was fond of making verses, but none have been preserved with the exception of some birthday lines composed when he was only thirteen years of age and addressed to his cousin, Maria Clark, afterwards Mrs. Macpherson, of Kingston, the mother of the author of Sir John's biography; and through her kindness they appeared as follows in the *Kingston Whig.*]

 The laughter-loving goddess Mirth,
 Whom lovely Venus at a birth,
 With two sister Graces more,
 To ivy-crowned Bacchus bore,
 To Scotia's Inverness once flew
 To sip the honey'd mountain dew;
 She there met Love, that wanton boy,
 Who does the hearts of youth annoy,
 And there resolved to form a mind
 With wit and loveliness combined.
 For this they got some white, clear clay,
 And then, before the dawn of day,
 They picked the wild flowers of the mount,
 And bathed their bosoms in a fount;
 With these they formed a beauteous frame,
 Well known for wit and mirth by fame;
 Mirth then found a lovely smile,
 And Cupid added a wanton wile;
 To these, the sigh which Pity wears,
 And Phaeton's pining sister's tears;
 All these, with clay our earthly part,
 Formed a feeling, laughing heart;
 To these were placed the ethereal spark,
 And from this rose Maria Clark.
      – J. A. M.

*Newspaper clipping, December 11, 1895, Public Archives of Canada.*

John A. Macdonald's Early Home, Hay Bay, Adolphustown, Bay of Quinte
'It was a clapboard wooden house, painted red, with a wooden shingled roof, the west half of the place being used as a store and the east as a dwelling.'

Canniff Haight, *Country Life in Canada Fifty Years Ago*

7

# John A. on Trial

John A. came to Picton in 1833 to manage Lowther Macpherson's law practice. The village was called Hallowell then, though its rival, Picton, was just across a small stream. In fact, one of John A.'s early activities was to join a group favouring Port William as the name of the combined rival settlements. He was also first secretary of the Prince Edward District School Board.

A fight between the young lawyer and Dr. Thomas Moore brought both of them to court in October 1834. Both were tried for assault, and the juries and their decisions are found in the 'Minutes of Quarter Sessions, Prince Edward District, April 1, 1834, to Jan. 6, 1835', a small manuscript volume in the Archives of Ontario. *The King versus Thomas Moore* resulted in a conviction and a fine of sixpence, while the case of *The King versus J. A. McDonald* (so spelled in the indictment) brought an acquittal.

The four witnesses for the prosecution of the future prime minister were David Barker, Henry J. Bonnycastle, Benjamin Hubbs, and Francis W. Smith; and it perhaps goes without saying that they would hardly be in line for political favours in the days to come.

Sir John always regretted his lack of higher education. He attended Kingston Grammar School for five years, leaving at age fifteen. 'If I had had a university education,' he once told Joseph Pope, his secretary, 'I should probably have entered upon the path of literature and acquired distinction therein.'

'I carried my musket in '37,' he recalled to his secretary. Like many another he joined a group setting out on foot for Toronto, the scene of the Rebellion. 'The day was hot, my feet were blistered – I was but a weary boy – and I thought I should have dropped under the weight of the flint musket which galled my shoulder. But I managed to keep up with my companion, a grim old soldier who seemed impervious to fatigue.'

Years after the Annexation Manifesto of 1849 Sir John spoke of the times in talking to his secretary: 'Our fellows lost their heads. I was pressed to sign it, but refused, and advocated the formation of the British America League as a more sensible procedure. . . . Our first resolution was that we were resolved to maintain inviolate the connection with the mother country.' Included in the 'true solution' was Confederation and a commercial national policy.

Main Street, Picton

In 1833-5 Macdonald was in charge of the Macpherson law office in Picton, in the upper storey of the frame building at the extreme left.

Macdonald's Home, Rideau Street, Kingston
He lived here in the early 1830s.

# We Must Send Him to the House

Those were the days of exclusiveness and snobbery, when it was almost as difficult to approach the august person of a Dodson or a Fogg as the Sleeping Beauty overhung with alarm bells and guarded by fiery dragons. . . . But no client, however poor, came out of Mr. Macdonald's office complaining of snobbery; rather telling of the courteous and gentlemanly young lawyer, 'quick as a flash', who understood his case better than the client himself before he had 'half told it'. In those days . . . when a young man discovered brilliant talents, or the power by his eloquence to carry his hearers, his friends invariably said, 'We must send him to the House'. We are told that in many a case which Mr. Macdonald pleaded, even strangers in the Courts, not knowing the young lawyer but observing his grasp of principles, the ease with which he led up all his arguments, and the power he had of compelling juries to take, by sympathy as well as by reason, his view of the case, were heard to exclaim 'The House is the place for him! . . .'

During the elections for the first parliament under the [Act of] Union the strife was high and confusion general. One day, sitting among friends in his office, Mr. Macdonald said, 'If I were only prepared now I should try for the Legislature,' and then added 'but it does no harm to wait.' The removal of the theatre of politics to his own city [Kingston] in 1841, gave impetus to his yearnings for political life; and thereafter he began to equip himself for the sphere in which he longed to move. But he did not, like too many empty young men of our own day, go noising through the country to attract the people's notice; he did not, indeed, woo the constituency at all, but decided to have the constituency woo him. . . . He attended much to the debates of the House, and . . . was profoundly engaged in preparing himself for his ideal sphere. While most of those who knew him thought his ambitions bent towards legal distinction only, he was acquiring that knowledge of constitutional, political, and parliamentary history which so early in his public career gave weight to his opinions and standing to himself.

*J. E. Collins*, The Life and Times of the Rt. Hon. Sir John A. Macdonald *(Toronto, 1883), pp. 50-2.*

His secretary and early biographer, Sir Joseph Pope, noted how fond Sir John was of the Kingston region, with treasured memories of Adolphustown, the Stone Mills, and Hay Bay. 'It is hard to tell what is your native place,' he once said to him. 'That's just what the Grits say,' rejoined Sir John. 'The *Globe* has it that I am born in a new place every general election.'

# John A., Champion of Unpopular Causes

Macdonald, who had carried a musket in militia drills during the Rebellion excitement, did not share the spirit of malice and repression which characterized the old-line Family Compact Tories of the period. As a lawyer, in fact, he took cases which in the eyes of many admitted of no defence and even tainted his reputation.

The escape of Rebellion prisoners from Fort Henry on the night of July 29, 1838, was speedily denounced as an inside job, and John Ashley, the jailer, was immediately arrested by the military under Colonel Dundas with no evidence whatever that he was implicated. Ashley was soon released but he entered suit against the Colonel, with Macdonald as one of his counsel. In the inflamed times, with Family Compact prosecutors lined up against him, Macdonald attacked with vigour the plain evidence of authoritarian extremism, and, though

Mr. Justice McLean summed up against his case, *Ashley vs. Dundas* was decided by the jury in the complainant's favour with £200 damages.

A few months later, after the piratical border raid of American Patriot Hunters at Windmill Point, Prescott, Macdonald similarly took the unpopular side in the court martial trial of the prisoners when, within the close limits of any type of defence in the circumstances, he assisted the leader, Von Schoultz, and Daniel George, who had a brother-in-law in Kingston, in their efforts to question the legality of the charges and otherwise to mitigate their almost defenceless conduct. Both men, and several others, were hanged, but Macdonald retained to the end of his life a vivid memory of his short association with Von Schoultz, who had been a Polish patriot before coming to America.

These cases were definite indications that as a Conservative, Macdonald would fight for liberal principles. His actions, in fact, foreshadowed a moderate conservatism when he was to become prominent in political life.

Sir Joseph Pope, *The Day of Sir John Macdonald*

# John A.'s First Marriage

On September 1, 1843, Macdonald . . . married his cousin, Isabella Clark. . . . A little later, when the bridegroom and his bride had returned from their honeymoon, they settled down in a house in Brock Street [Kingston],

John A. and Isabella Macdonald

J. P. Macpherson, *Life of Right Hon. Sir John A. Macdonald*

spacious and comfortable, replete with all the modern conveniences of a wonderful mechanical age. There was a library, for Macdonald had always bought and read books; there was a carriage and a pair of horses, 'Mohawk' and 'Charlie' . . .

[A year later his wife was suffering from frequent illnesses that were to continue and intensify until her death on December 28, 1858.] It was the expected, inevitable end for what had been for almost a dozen years a grey, unrelieved tragedy. Life had cheated him terribly; he had given everything where, in the very nature of the case, there could never be a full and satisfying response. By the two supreme efforts of her life, Isabella had borne children, one of whom had lived; but for years she had been a bedridden invalid, who was physically incapable of giving him the love, the support, and the companionship which he had craved. It was all over now – the agony of worry, the aching feeling of incompleteness, the patched habit of cheerful resignation. But for twelve years it had twisted his whole life. He had

Macpherson, *Life of Macdonald*

become a family man whose home was a hotel or a lodging-house; a bachelor husband who had to go for companionship to bars and lounges and smoking-rooms; a frustrated host who drank too much on occasion, partly because it was the only way he could entertain, and because it passed the empty time, and because it was an easy way to forget.

*Donald Creighton*, John A. Macdonald: The Young Politician *(Toronto, 1952), pp. 91-2, 260-1.*

'Bellevue', Kingston

John and Isabella (Clark) Macdonald spent their early married life here in the 1840s. John A., like other Kingstonians, considered the house 'the most fantastic concern imaginable' and nicknamed it 'Pekoe Pagoda'.

15

## Running for Town Council

Young Macdonald now saw his opportunity coming, and so did his friends, for they waited upon him towards the close of the summer of 1843 and invited him to come out for election to the Kingston council. . . . An eye-witness of the election and a friend of Macdonald says: 'The contest was a fierce one. At every tavern you found crowds of persons drunk and fighting. Capt. Jackson was the candidate against Macdonald, and he had all the noisy and drunken Irishmen in town on his side. I was passing by one of the booths and I happened to hear a ruffian of a fellow named Sullivan plotting with a large crowd of his own description to go in and prevent Macdonald from speaking, and go through his supporters. They knew me well, and I told them I had my eye upon them. This prevented a great row. I went in and found everybody inside fairly orderly, for Macdonald had a wonderful way of casting oil on troubled waters.' Jackson was overwhelmingly beaten.

*Collins*, Life of Macdonald, *p. 53.*

## First Election Manifesto, October 5, 1844

To the Free and Independent Electors of the Town of Kingston:

Gentlemen,

The approaching election calls upon me to redeem the pledge made in March last, in answer to the flattering requisition addressed to me by 225 electors, inviting me to become a candidate for the representation of this town.

A residence in Kingston since infancy has afforded every opportunity to me of knowing the wants and claims of our 'Loyal Old Town', and to you of ascertaining my political opinions, and my qualifications for the office I now solicit at your hands.

I, therefore, need scarcely state my firm belief that the prosperity of Canada depends upon its permanent connection with the Mother Country, and that I shall resist to the utmost any attempt (from whatever quarter it may come) which may tend to weaken that union.

The proposed measures for reducing the enormous expense of the public departments, for improving the system of common schools, and for opening and extending the advantages of our Collegiate Institute, will receive my cordial support.

It is alike my duty and my interest to promote the prosperity of this city and the adjacent country. No exertion will be spared by me in forwarding the settlement of our rear townships by the formation of public roads, in assisting and concentrating the trade of this port, and in such other local measures as will in any way conduce to your advantage.

I am deeply grateful for the confidence you have already reposed in me; and trusting that I have done nothing to forfeit it, I have the honour to be

Your obliged and faithful servant,

John A. Macdonald.

Public Archives of Canada

17

# The Election of 1844

The fury was not alone the property of the hustings during this campaign, but it blew a hurricane through the prints as well. Every editor dipped his pen in gall; every column reeked with libel. Those who had no newspapers issued handbills that might have fired the fences on which they were posted. . . . The contest came on in November, in a very hurricane of tumult. At more than one hustings blood was shed, and mutual massacre on a general scale only prevented by bodies of soldiers and special constables. The worst fiend known to man was loose in those days during the elections – the demon of whiskey. Near every booth were open houses where the excited mobs drank intoxicants furnished by the candidates till they became mad. For days before polling, ill-favoured-looking persons poured into Montreal, some carrying dirks and sling-shots and others pistols; . . . and in the riots gave many a bloody account of themselves. . . .

These were turbulent times in many parts of Upper and Lower Canada, and for several months preceding the elections monster meetings had been held by the party leaders at various parts of the province. It was not unusual to see proceeding to one of these gatherings a hundred teams, each carrying a dozen stalwart voters to stirring music, with flags flying, and every man armed with a club. Violent collisions often occurred, and the polling places were frequently the scenes of the maddest and most brutal party strife.

Of a similar character were the crowds that gathered at Kingston before the elections were held, some cheering for Mr. Manahan, others for Mr. Macdonald. Manahan was an Irishman, and all the bullies of the city were on his side. The number of these was comparatively small, but they could terrorize over a much larger number of peaceably disposed men. . . . Macdonald addressed several meetings in the open air, meetings composed of riotous men inflamed with whiskey and the worst passions of party. . . . 'Never,' says an eye-witness, 'did he lose temper, but good-naturedly waited till there were a lull in the disturbance.' When silence was restored, he said he knew most of the electors and they were all manly fellows – too manly, indeed, to refuse another fair play. . . . Here was something more than soothing speech; here, indeed, was the genius of a Mark Antony. . . . Every day the contest lasted saw his popularity grow and that of his opponent decrease, till, at length, a day before the polls closed, the latter rushed out of the field in despair, while in the midst of the wildest enthusiasm at the close Mr. Macdonald was carried through the city on a chair, the victor by an overwhelming majority of votes.

*Collins*, Life of Macdonald, *pp. 56-66.*

A Political Riot at St. Lawrence Hall, Toronto

# Pre-Confederation Politics

In 1854, when a bill was introduced in the old Parliament of Canada to create the city of Ottawa from old Bytown, a crude lumbering village, a discussion developed that did not reflect favourably on some who participated. John A., then Attorney General, took the view that it was absurd to call a town by the name of the river on which it was situated. 'How would it do,' he said, 'to call Paris "Seine" or London "Thames"?' George Brown aroused laughter when he said a move was then on foot to re-name Hamilton 'Ontario', and another member even suggested 'By-zantium' and 'By-copolis' as means of retaining the name of Colonel By. But who would think of objecting to 'Ottawa' today?

[In a debate in 1855 Macdonald twitted the Honourable George Brown with the favourable publicity he always gave himself, and the Grits in general, in his newspaper the *Globe*.]

'Whatever his colleagues did in the House, the hon. member for Lambton was sure to echo and applaud outside in the *Globe*. (Laughter.) When long lists of grants for St. Anne this or St. Anne that or St. Therese here or St. Therese there, were brought down by that Ministry, nothing could be better in the eyes of the hon. member for Lambton. "Look," he would say in that able journal of his, the *Globe* "how ministers take care to provide for education in Lower Canada, and how generously Upper Canadians vote the money for that great object."

'Later still . . . at Brantford, whither his colleague, being a modest man, desired to go quietly and unostentatiously, the member for Lambton (Mr. Brown) trotted him out and paraded him before the eyes of Upper Canada Liberals in a coach drawn by six white horses (an hon. member near me says Brown horses!). . . . During the late elections the *Globe* came out with the cry – "Down with Rolph and Malcolm Cameron! We can stand anything else – we can stand Toryism, we can stand Sir Allan McNab and John A. Macdonald, but we cannot stand Rolph. Corrupt may be Sir Allan McNab and steeped to the chin in Toryism, and John A. Macdonald may be following in his footsteps, a budding Tory at least they are not bad fellows, however, for Tories – but put down Rolph and Cameron." '

*Biggar*, Anecdotal Life, *pp. 70-1.*

# The Double Shuffle, 1858

The new parliament [with Macdonald-Cartier in power] assembled in February. The opposition [under George Brown] was in a more tumultuous state than ever, and this condition was due to the announcement that, on the recommendation of hon. John A. Macdonald and his colleagues, Ottawa . . . was chosen as the capital. . . .

After the ministry had got this troublesome question off its hands, a resolution and several amendments disapproving of her majesty's choice of Ottawa as a capital were moved by Messrs. Brown, Thibaudeau, Dunkin, Piché, and others. After an animated discussion Mr. Piché's amendment, setting forth that 'It is the opinion of this house that the city of Ottawa ought not to be the permanent seat of government for the province [of Canada]' was carried by a vote of sixty-four to fifty. Before the word 'carried' had left the speaker's lips George Brown's enthusiasm had passed bounds, and he jumped to his feet. 'The house', he said, as soon as the cheering ceased, 'can have no doubt that the motion just carried expressed an emphatic disapproval of the government policy; and in order to prove that it means just this, I now move an adjournment of the house.'

The premier [Macdonald] arose perfectly cool, and informed members that he was glad to accept the challenge of the leader of the opposition. 'Let the vote on adjournment', he said with a slightly ironical tone, 'test whether or not the ministry possesses the confidence of the house. . . .' When the speaker put the motion to adjourn . . . Macdonald was not mistaken. Sixty-one said 'nay' and only fifty 'yea'. . . . It was then agreed that the government could strike a decisive blow at the opposition by resigning. [The governor general, Sir Edmund Head, wrote to Brown offering him the opportunity to form a new administration, but would not dissolve parliament. Brown accepted and formed a ministry, but was at once defeated on a vote of non-confidence, and the Conservatives were back in power eight days after they had resigned. To be within the letter of a law passed the year before, all cabinet ministers were changed into different offices, so no election was necessary.] This was the expedient that has been since known as the 'double shuffle'. . . . The [Macdonald-Cartier] resignation was voluntary; but we must be frank enough to admit that it was not done out of deference to any principle or to the sense of the majority of the Upper Canada section of the cabinet. It was simply done to lure Mr. Brown into a pitfall; and into the pitfall he went, eyes and mouth wide open.

*Collins,* Life of Macdonald, *pp. 207-23.*

'The great reason why I have always been able to beat Brown', Sir John said in a letter to Sir John Rose (March 5, 1872), 'is that I have been able to look a little ahead, while he could on no occasion forgo the temptation of a temporary triumph.'

George Etienne Cartier

Charles Gill,
Public Archives of
Canada

# John A. Gives a Ball

On Valentine's day, February 14, 1860, Mr. Macdonald entertained all his friends at a ball, the magnificence of which is said to have never been surpassed in the city of Quebec. It was given in the Music Hall, then claimed to be the most beautiful room in British America; but on this occasion its usual attractions were supplemented by tasteful decorations and designs especially prepared for the occasion.

The room was brilliantly lighted, to insure which a handsome chandelier had been especially procured and suspended from the centre of the ceiling. Around the upper walls, above the gallery, had been hung graceful festoons of crimson drapery, looped at intervals by pendants of roses and evergreens.

Below the galleries, facing each other, were two alcoves, in one of which dwelt a life-sized Cupid who, as the god of love and valentines, smiled approval of the manner of celebrating the day. In the opposite alcove was placed a copy of Canova's celebrated statue of the 'Dancing Girl'. Near the entrance were the three Graces bearing a chaplet of beautiful flowers.

The stage, carpeted and balustraded with chains of choice flowers, was draped and overhung with materials in rose colour and white, with a view to present the appearance of a tent. In front was a large bust of Her Majesty, and near by a fountain of eau de Cologne. In the vicinity were placed sofas and lounges, amongst which were interspersed statuettes and small evergreen trees. The orchestra was adorned with flags, the Royal Arms, Prince of Wales plume, and other devices.

During the evening Mr. Macdonald, intent upon pleasing his guests in every possible manner, caused an immense amount of fun and enjoyment by distributing, with the aid of the stewarts [stewards] who acted for him, some hundreds of valentines for the particular benefit of the ladies. When supper came there was another surprise in the form of a large *pâté* from which, when opened, there flew out four and twenty birds, in imitation of those spoken of in history. There were about eight hundred guests present, and the ball was kept up until an early hour the next morning.

*J. P. Macpherson,* Life of the Right Hon. Sir John A. Macdonald *(Saint John, N.B., 1891), I, pp. 393-4.*

Ball at the Music Hall of the St. Louis Hotel, Quebec City

# The Visit of the Prince of Wales, 1860

[During the visit of the Prince of Wales to Canada in 1860, the Orange Order wished to parade in his honour in their regalia, but the Prince's secretary, the Duke of Newcastle, a Roman Catholic, refused to permit it. Kingston and Belleville were consequently omitted from the itinerary, and there was lesser trouble in Toronto. His efforts at peace-making being of no effect, John A. stayed at Kingston with its outraged citizens and took no further part in the Prince's reception. In an address that autumn he explained what took place.]

. . . When His Royal Highness came he was accompanied by the Duke of Newcastle, his constitutional adviser. Now I must say I think it unfortunate that the Prince was advised by the Duke of Newcastle. . . . . He did look upon things from an Imperial point of view, and, from his course upon the Orange question, I am quite certain that the Duke of Newcastle thought more of the condition and prospects of the Palmerston Government than of the Province. . . . He evidently never thought of the effect of his course upon Canada. . . . I believe the letter he wrote to the Mayor of Kingston was most injudicious and dictatorial. I am satisfied that had he made that request in the name of the Prince, that the Orangemen would not appear in badges and regalia, . . . there would have been no difficulty. (Cheers.) It is one thing to lead a man by kindness and courtesy, and another to shake a halter and say, 'Come along!' (Laughter and applause.) . . .

The Prince had reached Ottawa when the news arrived that there was likely to be difficulty at Kingston. Of course, I was exceedingly anxious that everything should pass over well at that place; and therefore, while His Royal Highness went up the Upper Ottawa, I left for Prescott for the purpose of meeting a deputation sent specially down to come to some arrangement with the Duke of Newcastle. I accompanied them back and introduced them to His Grace, with whom they had a long, earnest, and animated conversation on the matter. We pressed, in stronger and more emphatic language than His Grace was probably accustomed to hear, what we thought it was his duty to do, and what might be the consequence if he persisted in his threatened course. . . . His Grace said – and I am exceedingly grieved that he persisted in the course – 'As the Prince of Wales may visit Ireland next year, I cannot and will not advise him to take a course here that he cannot take there.' For this determination and the results of it the Duke of Newcastle alone is responsible.

*Macpherson*, Life of Macdonald, *I, pp. 398-408.*

The Prince of Wales at Dundurn Castle, Hamilton, 1860
With Sir Edmund and Lady Head, Sir Allan and Lady MacNab and others.

# Separate Schools and Orangemen

. . . As far as my own opinions are concerned, I am decidedly in favour of the continuance of the Separate School clause, and I will tell you the reason. As a Protestant, I should not like, if I ever lived in Lower Canada, to be obliged to send my child to a school of which the teacher was a Roman Catholic, and perhaps a Roman Catholic clergyman. (Hear, hear.) It is the duty of a religious teacher, if he believes anything to be true, to try to enforce it on the belief of his pupils. It is the duty of a sincere Protestant clergyman to try to proselytize every Roman Catholic. It is the duty of every sincere Roman Catholic to try to impress on others what he believes to be right. As an ardent Protestant who conscientiously believes that Protestantism and truth are one, I would not willingly subject my son to the chance of being turned by its teachers into what I consider wrong. (Applause.) And I appreciate the like feeling among my Roman Catholic brethren. (Renewed applause.) Why, the Catholics and the Protestants do not even read history alike. We look at the reigns of Henry VIII, Mary, and Elizabeth from one point of view – they from quite a different one. . . .

*Address at London, Canada West, 1860.*

Macdonald joined the Orange Order in 1841, though he was never active in it, if indeed he ever attended a meeting. When asked in 1861 why he joined he gave this answer:

'How did I become an Orangeman? I was not an Irishman by birth, and had little to do with politics in those days. It was in 1841, in times when Orangemen were on the descent, when the Provincial Legislature had proscribed them, forbidding them to wear their regalia and declaring their procession illegal; and at a time when they were about to pass a law preventing an Orangeman from becoming a juror or a constable, or holding any position under the Crown, thus branding him as an outlaw and a traitor to his country. . . . I resolved that if they – among whom were many of my best friends – were to be proscribed and hounded down merely because they were Orangemen, I would go in with them and submit to the same obloquy. Then, sir, I became an Orangeman.' [The legislation referred to was the Secret Societies Bill of 1843.]

*Biggar*, Anecdotal Life, *p. 113.*

Mr. M. C. Cameron: 'I would ask the Hon. Atty. Gen. West [John A. Macdonald], did he support Mr. Dunkin's Temperance Bill?'

Hon. J. A. Macdonald: 'I don't remember. I don't generally go for temperance bills.' (Laughter.)

28

*Canadian Illustrated News*

'Motion of non-confidence carried.'
The Legislative Assembly Meeting in Quebec City, May 1863
John A. Macdonald is in the front row just left of centre.

## George Brown and Confederation

On the day after the ministerial defeat [June 14, 1864] Mr. Brown fell into conversation with Messrs. J. H. Pope and Alexander Morris, supporters of the ministry. . . . He gave it as his opinion that a crisis had arrived . . . [and] expressed his willingness to coöperate with the existing or any other ministry that would deal promptly and firmly with the matter. The two ministerialists . . . asked if they might repeat the conversation to the conservative leaders. He readily consented, and the result was that on Friday the 17th Messrs. John A. Macdonald and A. T. Galt waited on Mr. Brown at his rooms in the St. Louis Hotel [Quebec], stating that they were authorized by the ministry to invite the coöperation of the liberal leader, with a view to the settlement of differences existing between Upper and Lower Canada. . . . The grit chief then intimated that 'it was quite impossible that he could be a member of any administration at present. . . .' In reply Mr. Macdonald said he considered it essential that Mr. Brown should be a member of the cabinet to give guarantees to the opposition and the country of the earnestness of the government. To do justice to Mr. Brown, he did not show any hopeless opposition to the proposal that he should enter the ministry, but suggested that all questions of a personal nature, and the necessary guarantees, might be waived for the present, 'and the discussion conducted with a view of ascertaining if a satisfactory solution of the sectional difficulty [between Canada East and Canada West] could be agreed upon'. He then requested to know what steps the government proposed towards settling sectional troubles. Promptly Messrs. Macdonald and Galt informed him that their remedy was 'a federal union of all the British North American provinces. . . .' With this plan Mr. Brown expressed himself dissatisfied. . . . As there is an impression among several writers that Mr. Brown was the parent of confederation, and entered the coalition for the purpose of forwarding the scheme, it may be as well to dispel the illusion. . . . The utmost credit, then, to which Mr. Brown is entitled is, not that he brought the union into life, but that he permitted its birth. Quite a different parent had the scheme. To use *Bystander's* [Goldwin Smith's] apt epigram, 'The father of confederation was dead-lock.'

*Collins*, Life of Macdonald, *pp. 281-3.*

George Brown
John C. Forbes, Ontario Parliament Buildings

*Canadian Illustrated News*

Torchlight Procession in Honour of George Brown, 1862

# Charlottetown Conference, 1864

As the Charlottetown Conference was informal and conversational, and intended to be secret, the verbal proposals during its meetings became known only in part and usually in reminiscences long after the event. No resolutions were adopted – except that to adjourn to Quebec – and no minutes of any type were kept.

When the Canadian political delegation arrived on the steamer *Victoria*, the receptions at Saint John, Halifax, and Charlottetown were both cordial and highly liquid. Seafood, champagne, and twelve-course dinners occupied many an afternoon and evening, with discussions and debates on union of any kind filling but a very minor place.

Charlottetown hotels were numerous but small, and when John A. and his fellow-delegates reached the Prince Edward Island capital in September the attractions of a circus had pretty well exhausted the accommodation. So the *Victoria* anchored, and the provincial secretary for Prince Edward Island, W. H. Pope, got a fisherman to row him out in an oyster boat, with a barrel of flour at one end and two big jars of molasses at the other – no doubt for ballast.

The rather general opposition to Maritime Union paved the way for the larger project. Macdonald and Cartier led off on general matters, with Cartier emphasizing French needs. A proposed senate of sixty members presented no difficulties. There were to be twenty from each of Canada East and Canada West, and twenty from the Maritimes, but their method of election or appointment was left for subsequent settlement. On the second day A. T. Galt spoke effectively on debts, subsidies, and other financial problems, including the money needed to buy out the island colony's absentee landlords. George Brown discussed the judiciary and constitutional details, and Cartier and Langevin favoured strong local legislatures when the division of power was to the fore. Later, at Halifax on September 12, agreement was reached to adjourn further discussion to October 10 at Quebec. Cartier was sure that it was either a union of the colonies or absorption into the United States. 'Everyone admits,' said Macdonald, 'that Union must take place sometime. I say now is the time.' And D'Arcy McGee made it still more emphatic, 'If we do not avail ourselves of the present opportunity of forming a Union with our fellow colonists, we will never have another.'

Short visits to Fredericton and Saint John ended the Conference, and on the 16th the delegates finally separated. The occupied part of Newfoundland seemed too remote to warrant even an invitation to the Charlottetown Conference, but two delegates from the island came to Quebec.

Convention at Charlottetown, Prince Edward Island of delegates from the legislatures of Canada, New Brunswick, Nova Scotia, and Prince Edward Island to take into consideration the union of the British North American Colonies, September 1, 1864.

# The Happy Opportunity . . . of Founding a Great Nation

Attorney-General Macdonald moved 'That a humble Address be presented to Her Majesty, praying that She may be graciously pleased to cause a measure to be submitted to the Imperial Parliament for the purpose of uniting the colonies of Canada, Nova Scotia, New Brunswick, Newfoundland, and Prince Edward Island in one Government, with provisions based on certain Resolutions which were adopted at a Conference of Delegates from the said Colonies, held at the city of Quebec on the tenth of October, 1864. . . .

'When this union takes place we will be at the outset no inconsiderable people . . . and with a rapidly increasing population – for I am satisfied that under this union our population will increase in a still greater ratio than ever before – with increased credit – with a higher position in the eyes of Europe – with the increased security we can offer to immigrants, who would naturally prefer to seek a new home in what is known to them as a great country than in any one little colony or another – with all this I am satisfied that, great as has been our increase in the last twenty-five years since the union of Upper and Lower Canada, our future progress, during the next quarter of a century, will be vastly greater. (Cheers.) . . .

'I must apologize for having detained you so long – for having gone perhaps too much into tedious details with reference to the questions bearing on the Constitution now submitted to this House. – (Cries of "No, no!" and "Go on!") – In conclusion I would again implore the House not to let this opportunity to pass. It is an opportunity that may never recur. . . . If we do not take advantage of the time, if we show ourselves unequal to the occasion, it may never return, and we shall hereafter bitterly and unavailingly regret having failed to embrace the happy opportunity now offered of founding a great nation under the fostering care of Great Britain and our Sovereign Lady, Queen Victoria.' (Loud cheers, amidst which the honourable gentleman resumed his seat.)

Parliamentary Debates on the Subject of the Confederation of the British North American Provinces (Quebec, 1865), pp. 25-6.

The Delegates of the Provinces at the Quebec Conference, 1864

# The Bill, the Whole Bill, Nothing but the Bill

Hon. Atty. Gen. Macdonald [after outlining the concessions granted to enable full debate]: 'Well, the debate began, it has gone on now for three weeks since that postponement, and as my hon. colleague the Hon. Provincial Secretary has said, it has dragged on wearily, with no prospect of an early termination. And how have we been met by hon. gentlemen opposite? . . . They have deliberately trifled with the question and wasted the time of the House.'

Hon. Mr. Holton: 'No, no!'

Hon. Atty. Gen. Macdonald: 'The hon. gentleman as a man of honour cannot deny it, as a man of candour he cannot deny it; and if he should deny it, his character as a man of honour and candour would sink in the estimation of this House. (Hear, hear.) I say it distinctly that this was the plot of hon. gentlemen opposite, to delay the consideration of this subject. Their policy was to wait, like Micawber, for "something to turn up", to see what would happen favourable to them in New Brunswick, to learn what would be done in Nova Scotia, and to embrace every pretext of delay that presented itself. The hon. gentleman was playing, deliberately playing, a trick . . . and, sir, I should be unworthy of the character the hon. gentleman [Hon. Mr. Holton] gives me of being a good parliamentary strategist, if I allowed this plot of preventing the House coming to a vote to succeed. (Hear, hear.) . . . And I will at once inform the House that to vote that the main question be not put will throw Confederation over forever, and forever destroy the last hopes of a friendly junction between the colonies of British North America.' (Hear, hear.)

Hon. Mr. Holton: 'Why the last hopes?'

Hon. Atty. Gen. Macdonald: 'Because if we reject now the agreement come to by all the governments of all the provinces, we can never expect to get them to meet again to make another.'

[Finally, on March 13, 1865, four amendments were defeated by votes of 84 to 35, 79 to 31, 95 to 8, and 85 to 20; after which the main motion was agreed to on a division and the Address was read by Attorney General Macdonald. On the following day it was transmitted to the Governor General.]

Confederation Debates, *pp. 726-1032.*

Fathers of Confederation in London, Christmas Eve, 1866

# Architect of Confederation

Hon. Mr. Holton held that the Government ought to ask for an affirmative vote from the House on each of these resolutions [in the Address to the Queen praying for an Act of the British Parliament to enact Confederation].

Hon. A. A. Dorion said . . . that the freedom of Parliament would be better consulted, and more opportunity would be given to learn the sense of the House by the different clauses of the Address being moved *seriatim*, in the same way as supplies were voted.

Atty. Gen. Macdonald could understand the object of the hon. member for Hochelaga. The hon. gentleman was opposed to Confederation, and the course which he proposed was just that which was calculated to throw the scheme to another Parliament and till another conference was held, so that Confederation might not be effected till the day of judgment. These resolutions were in the nature of a treaty, and if not adopted in their entirety the proceedings would have to be commenced *de novo*. If each province undertook to change the details of the scheme, there would be no end to the discussions and the conferences which would have to be held.

Mr. Thomas Ferguson asked whether it was the intention of the Government to carry this measure into force without submitting it to the people?

Atty. Gen. Macdonald said he could answer his hon. friend at once. If this measure received the support of the House, there would be no necessity of going to the people. If, however, the measure were defeated, it would be for the Government to consider whether there should not be an appeal to the country. (Hear, hear, and laughter.)

Confederation Debates, *pp. 15-16.*

[During the Canadian debates on Confederation in 1865 Macdonald answered a member's objection that the confederated Canada, as a result of greater strength, would be more likely to withdraw from the Mother Country.]

'I believe it will have the contrary effect. I believe that as we grow stronger, that, as it is felt in England we have become a people, able from our union, our strength, our population, and the development of our resources, to take our position among the nations of the world, she will be less willing to part with us than she would be now. . . . The colonies are now in a transition state. Gradually a different colonial system is being developed – and it will become, year by year, less a case of dependence on our part, and of over-ruling protection on the part of the Mother Country, and more a case of a healthy and cordial alliance. . . . England will have in us a friendly nation – a subordinate, but still a powerful people – to stand by her in North America in peace or in war.' (Cheers.)

Confederation Debates, *pp. 43-5.*

J. W. Bengough, Rapid Grip and Batten Ltd.

Confederation! The Much-Fathered Youngster
(Left to right) George Brown, Sir Francis Hincks, William McDougall, and Sir John A. Macdonald.

# UNION DAY.

## Proceedings at the Privy Council Chambers.

According to previous announcement the Judges assembled at the Privy Council Chambers, along with the members of the extinct Canadian Government, and the Ministers from the Maritime Provinces before eleven o'clock. A large number of gentlemen had previously gathered in the corridor, and anxiously awaited the opportunity to witness the ceremony of swearing in LORD MONCK as the first GOVERNOR-GENERAL of CANADA, in its enlarged sense, according to the Union Act.

A few minutes after eleven o'clock VISCOUNT MONCK, attended by his Secretary, Mr. GODLEY, drove up to the Departmental building in Mr. Buckley's carriage. HIS EXCELLENCY was dressed in plain clothes, and entered the building almost before the crowd had noticed his presence, and without any demonstration on the part of the people...

Mr. DENIS GODLEY then read HER MAJESTY'S commission to VISCOUNT MONCK, appointing him GOVERNOR-GENERAL OF HER MAJESTY'S DOMINION OF CANADA, and reciting at length the authority with which he was invested, by which all HER MAJESTY'S powers, and prerogatives within the said Dominion are delegated to him, with the further power of delegating all or such of them in one or any of the Provinces as he may from time to time see fit, and further providing in case of his absence from the country, death, or incapacity, for the appointment of an administrator...

### Honors to the Delegates.

Not an inkling had reached the public ear of what was next to follow. It was even stated afterwards that Ministers themselves were not aware of the gracious intention of her Majesty to confer upon them such a distinguished mark of the Royal favor.

His Excellency being seated, spoke to the following effect :

I have instructions from her Majesty's Secretary of State for the Colonies, to announce that her Majesty has been pleased, in recognition of the distinguished services of the Hon. JOHN A. MACDONALD, especially with reference to the accomplishment of Confederation, and as President of the Colonial Conference in London, to bestow upon him a mark of her Royal favor. Her Majesty has therefore been pleased to confer upon the Hon. JOHN A. MACDONALD, the title of KNIGHT COMMANDER OF THE MOST HONORABLE ORDER OF THE BATH. (Cheers.)

HIS EXCELLENCY continued--I have further to state that, in recognition of the like services, HER MAJESTY has been further pleased to confer the title of COMPANION of the BATH upon the Hon. Mr. HOWLAND, the Hon. Mr MACDOUGALL, the Hon. Mr. CARTIER, the Hon. Mr. GALT, the Hon. Dr. TUPPER, and the Hon. Mr. TILLEY. (Applause.) HIS EXCELLENCY said that in distributing these honors HER MAJESTY'S Government desired it to be understood that the same distinction had been observed as that established by the Conference of Delegates at London—the three divisions, Upper Canada, Lower Canada, and the Maritime Provinces had each been treated as a unit, and HER MAJESTY had, following the same distinction, distributed these honors to two of the representatives of each division.

The public were then requested to retire, when we understand the formation of the new Government was immediately proceeded with, and the Privy Council sworn in. His EXCELLENCY came out at noon to witness the review on Parliament Square, and again returned to the Privy Council, where he remained with the Ministers up to nearly six o'clock. It was generally understood that all the Bureaus had been assigned, and the Lieutenant-Governors appointed before the Council adjourned—not a bad day's work for the FIRST UNION DAY.

### The Celebration in the City.

As we mentioned on Monday morning the UNION was ushered in at midnight by the firing of one hundred and one guns, the kindling of a bon-fire on the Ordnance lands opposite the Cathedral, the ringing of bells and the discharge of fireworks.

*Ottawa Times*, July 3, 1867, J. Alex. Edmison Collection

Proclamation of Confederation in Market Square, Kingston, July 1, 1867

# Sir John Guides the Nation

[Read by the Governor General, Viscount Monck, this Speech from the Throne was probably in large part composed by Sir John A. Macdonald, who, with his brother-in-law Hewitt Bernard,* drew up as well most of the British North America Act.]

'Hon. Gentlemen of the Senate – Gentlemen of the House of Commons:

'In addressing for the first time the parliamentary representatives of the Dominion of Canada, I desire to give expression to my own deep feeling of gratification that it has been my high privilege to occupy an official position which has made it my duty to assist at every step taken in the creation of the great Confederation. . . .

'With the design of effecting these objects, measures will be laid before you for the amendment and assimilation of the laws now existing in the several provinces relating to currency, custom, excise, and revenue generally; for the adoption of a uniform postal system; for the proper management and maintenance of public works and the properties of the Dominion; for the adoption of a well considered scheme of militia organization and defence; for the proper administration of Indian affairs; for the introduction of uniform laws respecting patents of invention and discovery; the naturalization of aliens, and the assimilation of the criminal law and the laws relating to bankruptcy and insolvency. A measure will also be submitted to you for the performance of the duty imposed upon Canada under the terms of the Union Act of immediately constructing the Intercolonial Railway. This great work will add a practical and physical connection to the legislative bond which now unites the provinces comprising the Dominion; and the liberality with which the guarantee for the cost of its construction was given by the Imperial Parliament is a new proof of the hearty interest felt by the British people in your prosperity.

'Your consideration will also be invited to the important subject of western territorial extension, and your attention will be called to the best means for the protection and development of our fisheries and marine interests.

'You will also be asked to consider measures defining the privileges of Parliament and for the establishment of uniform laws relating to elections and the trial of contested elections.'

*Toronto* Leader, *November 8, 1867.*

*On February 16, 1867, while Macdonald was at the London Conference, he married Susan Agnes Bernard, sister of his long-time associate, Hewitt Bernard.

Contested elections because of bribery and corruption were frequent in the days of oral voting and a small electorate, but they did not immediately end when vote by ballot was introduced. In 1887 both Sir John and the Leader of the Opposition, the Honourable Edward Blake, sat in the House for two constituencies, 'pending the trial of petitions to void their respective elections'.

Alfred Jones, *Harper's Weekly*

Opening of the First Parliament of the New Dominion of Canada

# First Parliament after Confederation

There was no fanfare when the first Parliament of the Dominion assembled in Ottawa in November 1867; no grand opening address by Sir John Macdonald inaugurated the new government – in fact he kept definitely in the background, allowing others to make the long speeches while he directed the proceedings, saw that the right precedents were set, and smoothed out difficulties with a master hand. The only change was that 'John A.' had become 'Sir John A.' in recognition of his pre-eminent part in the achievement of Confederation.

Before legislation could be brought before the House and Senate, Speakers had to be elected, procedures set up, the payment of members fixed, and standing committees appointed. Sir John often moved these resolutions, but let others do the debating. He moved, seconded by the Hon. George Cartier, that the Hon. James Cockburn (West Northumberland, Ontario) be the Speaker of the House. Here is what immediately followed.

M. Dufresne (Montcalm) opposed Mr. Cockburn's appointment on the ground that he did not understand French. Both languages were on the same footing, and it would be unsatisfactory to the French population if all the proceedings were conducted in the English language as they just had been in the Senate.

M. Cartier in reply said Mr. Cockburn did understand French, though perhaps he did not speak it with the facility of the member for Montcalm. The House had before had Speakers not speaking French very fluently, as Sir Allan MacNab, Sir Henry Smith, and Mr. Sandfield Macdonald, and nobody had complained.

The motion being put was carried unanimously.

To keep a balance in the race problem, the Hon. J. Cauchon was elected Speaker of the Senate.

Sir John suggested that $6 per day be set as payment of members, with $600 as the sessional indemnity, assuming a session of about ninety days. Each member would also receive 6d. or 10 cents a mile (both currencies were in use at the time) for travel expenses, but this included meals and accommodation en route. The absence of members from the House cost them $5 per day deduction. There was lengthy discussion about these amounts, particularly from those farthest away from Ottawa, in Nova Scotia and New Brunswick. Some wanted to be able to put in expense accounts for approval, but the Prime Minister had a humorous reply:

Sir John: 'The accounts would be contested, and it might afterwards be thrown in the face of a member on the hustings by an opposing candidate that in going to the seat of government he had travelled more like a prince than a representative of homespun people in the backwoods. Members, also, would be looking at what the others had charged before they make their declaration.' (Laughter.)

There was a lengthy debate on the Speech from the Throne, with each paragraph debated separately and eventually approved. But Joseph Howe of Nova Scotia was hostile and wanted to move an amendment deprecating the adoption of Confederation without its submission first to the people of his province; he said, however, he knew it would go through whatever he did, and

45

finally withdrew his amendment. A French member, M. Desaulniers, seconded Mr. Fisher's motion of adoption of the address, congratulating the House and the country on Confederation, which, he said, 'gave his countrymen the best safeguard for their peculiar national interests'.

It was decided that there was to be no bar or service of liquor in the House, including the Speaker's chambers. There was to be provision for dinner to be served, and the Speaker arranged as well to give a series of receptions and 'social reunions' for the members, which would serve, as the Honourable Sandfield Mac-donald put it, 'to smoothe down the asperities' of political life.

Mr. Fisher said that there was a great need to take over the West in some way or other, to develop its potentialities and place settlers there before some other country did; for as he put it, an American friend in Detroit told him that 'if you do not go up there pretty soon, we will squat you out.' The 'Fenian scare' came in for mention as well, and there was no doubt that the members appreciated the difficulties to be overcome.

One member took a rise out of the member for Cornwall, John Sandfield Macdonald, who

46

*Canadian Illustrated News*

had, he suggested, been buying old chairs and tables everywhere to use in Cornwall, which he had hoped would be selected as the capital of Canada, or at least the site of some government buildings. Sir John, sensing the opportunity for a quip, said that 'if the proposition were to be carried out he hoped his hon. friend from Cornwall would give his services to select the furniture'. (Laughter.)

[The proceedings of the first Parliament, and for several years afterwards, were not printed. The newspapers, however, reported them fully, the Toronto *Leader* being the basis of this account.]

The lobby of the old Russell House, Ottawa, long a favourite hangout for Members of Parliament, lawyers, and political manipulators.

# Better Terms For Nova Scotia

The general election for the House of Commons was held during the summer and early autumn. Quebec and Ontario emphasized their approval of union and coalition by returning overwhelming majorities of ministerialists; and George Brown was defeated in South Ontario. . . . Though the dark-age organs and the 'anti' politicians of New Brunswick had waged bitter war against all who had favoured union, the ministry there carried twelve of the fifteen seats. Nova Scotia had been caught by a counter breeze and driven back from her late position. Dr. Tupper had worsted Joseph Howe before the imperial ministers [at the London conference] but the latter had the *post mortem* victory before the province. For once the sturdy doctor found that neither his lungs nor his courage were sufficient against the stream of burning eloquence that flowed from the 'Great Anti'. The battle for the confederates was another Flodden, one man only – and he Dr. Tupper – reaching Ottawa with a tattered flag. Eighteen sturdy antis were sent up from the distant peninsula to the first dominion parliament. . . . No one doubts that the great Nova Scotian orator was a sincere patriot, but like some other clever men he possessed in no little degree a sense of self-importance which sometimes dimmed or distorted his vision. . . .

In July [1868] . . . Sir John Macdonald suggested to his colleagues the propriety of some members of the cabinet attending the conference to be held in Halifax in August. . . . They reasoned, expostulated, offered to investigate every grievance and as far as possible to remedy the same; but the antis were not to be comforted. . . . [He] offered to revise the conditions of Nova Scotia's connexion with the confederation, and invited Joseph Howe to a seat in the ministry. Mr. Howe . . . gave way,

and in January of the new year, 1869, entered the government as president of the council. At a cabinet meeting the details of the 'Better Terms' sought for Nova Scotia were determined: Canada undertook to assume $9,186,756 of the provincial debt instead of $8,000,000 as originally fixed, and to grant an annual subsidy of $82,698 for ten years.

*Collins*, Life of Macdonald, *pp. 339-50.*

48

Joseph Howe

## Red River Rebellion

[April 6, 1870]
Sir John A. Macdonald: '. . . I have simply to state that we have no further intelligence, but the intelligence is complete as to the fact of the man [Thomas Scott] having been shot by a party of men calling themselves a Court Martial. That the man was murdered there can be no doubt. . . . I may say that the two Governments are acting in accord and unison – (hear, hear) – and with the one object in view, that of retaining that country as a portion of Her Majesty's Dominions and of restoring law and order therein. . . . What that line of conduct may be, must be for the present withheld from the House. . . .'

Alexander Mackenzie: 'Then does the Government intend to delay active proceedings in the meantime?'

Sir John A. Macdonald: 'I have told my hon. friend that the two Governments are quite in accord, and that our policy is one of action – (cheers) – and I think my hon. friend ought to be satisfied with that. . . .'
[May 2, 1870]

Sir John A. Macdonald: 'I rise, sir, with the consent of the House, to submit the result of our deliberations for the framing of a constitution for the country heretofore known as Rupert's Land and the North West Territory. . . . The name Assiniboia, by which it has hitherto been called, is considered to be rather too long, involving confusion, too, between the river Assiniboine and the Province Assiniboia. I suppose, therefore, there will be no objection to the name that has been fixed upon [Manitoba], which is euphonious enough in itself, and is an old Indian name, meaning "The God who speaks – the speaking God . . ." (Hon. Sir John A. Macdonald here placed a map on the table showing the boundaries of the new Province, and the members gathered round to examine it.) . . . 'I am glad to say that events have recently resulted in an arrangement . . . for the despatch of an expedition . . . comprised partly of Her Majesty's regular troops and partly of Canadian Militia . . . and the expenditure will be borne in the same proportion, Her Majesty's Government paying one-fourth of the expenditure and the Dominion three-fourths. My hon. friend beside me (Hon. Sir George E. Cartier) reminds me that since the written arrangement was entered into, which I have just mentioned, a proposition was made to increase Her Majesty's contingent by perhaps 140. . . . I now move the first reading of the bill.'

Debates of the House of Commons (Ottawa, 1870), I, cols. 898-903, 1287-1295.

Red River Expedition Portage
Frances Anne Hopkins, Public Archives of Canada

51

# Silence Is Golden

[Largely through British lack of interest in Canadian affairs, the terms of the Washington Treaty with the United States were highly prejudicial to Canadian interests. Sir John was the first Canadian to present an approach to a national view, but he was met with a superior and condescending attitude towards 'the colonies'. When he reluctantly signed the Treaty, he was heard to say in a low voice, 'Well, here go the fisheries!' Sir John's address of over four hours on the issue was one of his greatest in the House of Commons; the following excerpts are from the closing portion.]

'I have not said a word for twelve months. I have kept silence to this day, thinking it better that the subject should be discussed on its own merits. How eagerly was I watched! If the Government should come out in favour of the Treaty, then it was to be taken as a betrayal of the people of Canada. If the Government should come out against the Treaty, then the First Minister was to be charged with opposing the interests of the Empire. Whichever course we might take they were lying in wait, ready with some mode of attack. But 'silence is golden', Mr. Speaker, and I kept silence. I believe the sober second thought of this country accords with the sober second thought of the Government; and we come down here and ask the people of Canada through their representatives to accept this Treaty, to accept it with all its imperfections, to accept it for the sake of peace, and for the sake of the great Empire of which we form a part.

'I now beg leave to introduce the Bill, and to state that I have the permission of His Excellency to do so.'

The hon. gentleman resumed his seat at 9:45, after having spoken for four hours and a quarter, amid loud and continued applause from all parts of the House.

House of Commons Debates *(1873), III, pp. 293-345.*

[At the negotiations (1871) leading to the Treaty of Washington, during an official excursion on the Potomac to which he had come early and alone, the wife of an American senator fell into conversation with Sir John:]

'I guess you come from Canada?'

'Yes, ma'am.'

'You've got a very smart man over there, the Honorable John A. Macdonald.'

'Yes, ma'am, he is.'

'But they say he's a regular rascal.'

'Yes, ma'am, he's a perfect rascal.'

'But why do they keep such a man in power?'

'Well, you see, they cannot get along without him.'

'But how is that? They say he's a real skalawag, and . . .'

Just then her husband, the Senator, stepped up and said:

'My dear, let me introduce the Honorable John A. Macdonald.'

The lady's feelings can be imagined, but Sir John put her at her ease, saying: 'Now don't apologize! All you've said is perfectly true, and it is well known at home.'

*Biggar*, Anecdotal Life, *p. 196.*

The British High Commissioners, Washington, 1871
(Standing) the Secretary to the Commissioners, Sir John A. Macdonald, Montague Bernard,
(seated) Sir Stafford Northcote, Earl de Grey and Ripon, Sir Edward Thornton.

# The Workingman's Friend

Late in June 1872 John A. received a letter from the secretary of the Toronto Trades Assembly stating that the trades unions of Canada wished to make a presentation to Lady Macdonald 'as a slight token of our appreciation of your timely efforts in the interests of the operatives of this Dominion'. He accompanied her to the meeting, where she was given a handsome gold jewelled casket and an appreciative address. Reference was made to the Typographical Union and its efforts towards a 9-hour workday, and to the 'harsh and un-called-for' arrest of twenty-three printers – an arrest 'instigated by the proprietor of a newspaper whose animus leads him to follow, even to the death, those who cross his path'. This reference was obviously to George Brown of the *Globe,* and in Sir John's address of thanks on behalf of his wife*, he accepted the opportunity to offer another approach to labour problems. He promised 'respectful and prompt attention' to any representations made to him in the interests of labour legislation, and ended in that effective jocular style that served such a variety of purposes:

'I ought to have a special interest in this subject, because I am a working-man myself. I know that I work more than nine hours every day myself; and then I think that I am a practical mechanic. If you look at the Confederation Act, in the framing of which I had some hand, you will admit that I am a pretty good joiner; and as for cabinet-making, I have had as much experience as Jacques and Hay themselves.' And after all the cheering and hand-clapping that followed, Sir John and Lady Macdonald were drawn through the streets in a carriage, accompanied by an enthusiastic torch-light procession.

*Based on the report in the Toronto* Mail, *July 12, 1872.*

Sir John: . . . 'It was a dreadful thing to see, as I have seen in Toronto, operatives and mechanics working on three quarter and half time, while every auction room and commission shop was glutted with goods from the United States and sold at a sacrifice – the sweepings of shops in the Republic, after supplying their own wants, sent over here and sold at ruinous figures to crush out our infant industries and give our people no hope of fair competition. We said again and again our mechanics and artisans and manufacturers should have some protection against this state of affairs. We pressed it in Parliament; we pressed it through the newspapers advocating the same principles as ourselves; we pressed it from the platform and on the people. (Cheers.) And the people were with us. (Cheers.) They rose in their might in 1878 and most unmistakably, by their verdict, declared that they had weighed the Government of Mr. Mackenzie in the balance and found it wanting.' (Cheers and applause.)

*'Speech . . . to the Workingmen's Liberal Conservative Association of Ottawa and Le Cercle Lafontaine' (1886).*

---

*On another occasion when Lady Macdonald was asked to speak, at Brantford, she thanked her audience for welcoming her, and said: 'I need not tell you that I cannot make a speech. I leave speech-making to my husband, who, I am proud to think, can make very good ones.'

J. W. Bengough, *Canadian Illustrated News*

Toronto Workingmen Present Testimonial to Lady Macdonald

# Sir John and the 'Pacific Scandal'

[In October 1872 the Huntington charges claimed the discovery of evidence that Sir Hugh Allan and his supporters had received the charter to build the Canadian Pacific Railway in return for contributions to the Conservative campaign fund. It was a bombshell that caused ever-increasing consternation in that party, and the 'Pacific Scandal' was on every member's mind as the Reformers pushed relentlessly for investigation. Day after day Sir John Macdonald saw his majority in the House dwindling, as more and more Conservatives dropped away. He remained silent until it appeared obvious that too many of his own party would not continue to support him, and that defeat was inevitable; whereupon he rose from his seat on November 3 and for five and one-half hours covered every point at issue attempting valiantly under continual interruption to explain away the charges of political corruption. The Speaker said more than once that language was used on all sides that should not have been allowed. At times Sir John rose to flights of oratory in defence of his administration.]

I say this government has been treated with foul wrongs. (Cheers.) I say this government has been treated as no government in any civilized country was ever met. (Loud cheers.) I say we have been opposed not with fair weapons, not by fair arguments, not by fair discusssion, but opposed in a manner which will throw shame on hon. gentlemen opposite. (Renewed cheers.)

. . . I have fought the battle of Confederation, the battle of Union, the battle of the Dominion of Canada. I throw myself upon this House, I throw myself upon this country, I throw myself upon posterity, and I know that notwithstanding the many failings of my life, I shall have the voice of this country and this House rallying around me. (Cheers.) And, sir, if I am mistaken in that, I confidently appeal to a higher court – to the court of my own conscience and to the court of posterity. (Cheers.) I leave it with this House with every confidence. I am equal to either fortune. I can see past the decision of this House, either for or against me, but whether it be for or against me, I know – and it is no vain boast for me to say so – for even my enemies will admit that I am no boaster – that there does not exist in Canada a man who has given more of his time, more of his heart, more of his wealth, or more of his intellect and power, such as they may be, for the good of this Dominion of Canada. (Loud and prolonged cheers.)

[After the election was fought on the issue, Sir John was left with just 45 members out of a House of 206.]

House of Commons Debates, *November 3, 1872.*

"WE IN CANADA SEEM TO HAVE LOST ALL IDEA OF JUSTICE, HONOR AND INTEGRITY."—The Mail, 26th September.

J. W. Bengough, Rapid Grip and Batten Ltd.

# Elections and Democracy

In the days of nominations by a show of hands and elections by recorded oral ballot it was easy to see how the contest was going. In one election the show of hands favoured Macdonald so unanimously that some of his supporters broke away and supported the Opposition, for an acclamation would mean no election, and an election was not only a time of intimidation and bribery but one of jollification and heavy drinking, and as such was not to be missed.

Vote by ballot came before the House in the late eighteen forties, but Macdonald opposed it on the ground that 'the people of Canada have no one exercising an illegitimate influence over them as in England and European countries'.* The Conservative party, in fact, opposed manhood suffrage until near the close of the century, taking the view that the possession of property as well as the prestige of class should be the criterion of the right to vote.

John A. frequently opposed reforms, not so much because he was against them in principle but because he thought public opinion was not ready for them or had made no demand for them. Subsequently, under changed conditions, he would shape legislation of the type he had earlier rejected.

Even in the later part of Sir John's prominence, democracy, while not quite a dirty word, was a way of life commonly considered, as by Sir John himself, to be too extreme, too republican, and too American for Canada. He was a believer too in a somewhat restrained class system, with the Queen the *fons honoris* in granting titles. At one time he thought that all chief justices should be knighted.

When 'Rep by Pop' (Representation by Population) was being pressed by George Brown and the Grits in the eighteen-fifties, Macdonald and the Conservatives were not entirely against the principle but opposed it at the time to prevent the swamping of the French in Canada East. John A. said its development should come gradually, the Conservatives of the day believing that it was too democratic and might well break up the union of Canada East and Canada West whenever one or the other had a preponderant population.

Comments by Macdonald, some of them made in jocular mood, were none the less evidence of broadmindedness and a flexible attitude. For example, in 1886 he said he would do all he could for votes for women, though, of course, the times were not ripe for their political emancipation. The pages of history are full of 'men of strong faith and high principles', as they are usually called. But frequently they have been bigoted, self-righteous, and viciously uncompromising, as well as leaders in repression who did not scruple to put opponents and dissenters to death, both metaphorically and literally. If Sir John had been one of them his place in Canadian history would have been infinitesimal.

*New Brunswick had vote by ballot earliest, in 1855, but the old system persisted in elections for the House of Commons until 1874.

The Smoking-Room, House of Commons, 1872

Douglas Library, Queen's University

Author's collection

# Sir John in Opposition

[Both as a speaker and a humorist, Sir John not infrequently left something to be desired. But his sense of humour was infectious and his jokes sometimes passed current because he knew how to put them over. Indications are that he was a past-master in getting audiences in the mood of laughing, even before anything funny was said. The following excerpt from an address in Montreal in 1876, when he was in opposition, illustrates these characteristics in one of his less inspired efforts.]

... Our views may be wrong, but I say this, if you will read those speeches you will not find one word without its warrant. We attacked no private character; we never struck below the belt. (Enthusiastic cheers.) ... And, gentlemen, what said Mr. Mackenzie in response to these speeches? ... Was the tone worthy of the Premier of Canada? ... (Cries of oh! oh! big push, etc.) Mr. Mackenzie made the error that he always does, of mistaking coarseness for strength. (Cheers.) The Hon. Alex Mackenzie is a countryman of my own; he is a hard-headed Scotchman. He makes clear, well reasoned, logical speeches, but the gods have not made him poetical. He wants imagination, and though his speeches are sound and sensible, and able, they are I must say, upon the whole as dry as a limeburner's shoe. (Laughter and cheers.)

The other day he assumed a new character; he broke out in a new place (loud laughter), and for the first time in his life he favoured his audience with a poetical quotation. Now, it rather surprised me when he, the Puritan Premier, had the whole range of British poetry to quote from, that he had preferred to quote that rakehelly old cavalier, Sam Butler. (Laughter.) Poetry is called 'a garden of sweets', a 'garland of roses', either raising the imagination by the sublimity of the ideas, or charming the fancy by the beauty of the sentiments of the poet. Now, let us call to our memory the quotations made by the Hon. Alexander Mackenzie, which, mind you, he especially applies to the Opposition. It is this:

> The Prince of Cambay's daily food
> Is asp and basilisk and toad,
> Which gives to him so strong a breath,
> He nightly stinks a queen to death.

(Laughter.) You may judge, gentlemen, from this poetical outburst of the Premier of Canada, of the kind of answers we get in the House. We tell him 'Your Pacific policy is wrong.' He answers 'You are an asp.' (Loud laughter.) We tell him 'that the Tariff is a mistake.' 'You are a basilisk.' (Renewed laughter.) We say to him 'How about the steel rails?' 'You are a toad.' (Laughter.) I have seen him again and again in the House of Commons give answers polite as the answers I have been supposing at this moment.

Liberal Conservative Hand-Book, Grits in Office, *1876, pp. 5-6.*

Sheet Music in Honour of Sir John as
Leader of the Opposition, 1874

# Mucilage and Penknives

[Sir John was a great student of the proceedings of the British Parliament and often referred to them in the House. Once he recalled that it was the fashion in Lord Melbourne's day to swear and curse a good deal. The Reverend Sydney Smith, said Sir John, had a way of quietly but effectively interrupting Lord Melbourne's flow of curses with the comment: 'Now, my lord, let us consider everybody cursed and get down to business.' Continuing, Sir John developed an analogy with the current House.]

Sir John: 'Now, sir, let us consider that the late administration [Sir John's] is damned, not for all eternity, but for all time at any rate.'

Mr. Mackenzie: 'We do.'

Sir John: 'My hon. friend would look more pleasant if he thought that were going to be so. Let us consider that we have committed every sin in the calendar, from high treason down to the nuisances my hon. friend from Hamilton is going to deal with, and what then? The hon. gentlemen opposite have to answer for their own offences, not for ours. . . . I remember the time when there was a great cry throughout the country that my Administration had been guilty of all kinds of crimes because they had paid too much for mucilage and penknives. From every hustings, at every election, the cry of mucilage and penknives was raised against them, but a decent old Reformer said the other day in Ontario, "I don't know how it is Sir John managed the country with a little mucilage and a few penknives, when it takes millions of dollars to keep our own party in power." '

*Adapted from Biggar,* Anecdotal Life, *pp. 121-3.*

Sir John: 'Gentlemen, I have to ask you to move your boots pretty lively between now and the 20th of June. (Laughter and applause.) I have no fear of the result if you will work. Do not sleep; do not be too confident. I have said again and again that the two most uncertain things in the world are an election and a horse-race. (Laughter.) Don't let the Opposition horse beat the good N.P. [National Policy] nag by a nose. (Applause.) You must show your tail to the hindermost horse. (Hear, hear.) "Oh, purists never use money!" you say; but you surely cannot forget that one of the best supporters of the Grit party, H. H. Cook – a very good fellow – confessed to having spent in his own election as much as $28,000.'

A Voice: 'I bet you.'

Another Voice: 'And there was Walker.'

Sir John: 'Yes; the gentleman who wrote "Come along, John; let's put down bribery and corruption; I've lots of money".'

The Dominion Campaign! Sir John Macdonald on the Points at Issue before the People. The Premier's Great Speech before the Workingmen of Toronto, 1872 (*pamphlet*).

# Political Picnics

[In 1876, on Dominion Day to be precise, a new type of political meeting was inaugurated by the Conservatives – the picnic. It became increasingly important as the right to vote was extended, for at first the electorate was relatively small and based on property, and a selective franchise was long a policy of John A. and his party.

The first political picnic was at Uxbridge, and included with John A. and his wife Agnes among the notabilities were John Beverley Robinson, Charles Tupper, and William Mc-Dougall. Part of the festivities was lunch, varying from all the substantials and delicacies of the season for the notables, to whatever you brought with you for the rest. The addresses followed. Even a heavy shower did not dampen the enthusiasm.

But the best part was his mixing with the common people, 'a cross-section of the nation, a sample of town and village and countryside'.]

They were all there [says his biographer] – from the elegant young barrister with his brocaded waistcoat and fashionably checked trousers, who had come out in the train from Toronto, to the thick-set, bearded farmer from Greenbank or Blackwater in his sagging 'best' black coat and rusty top hat. Here was the wife of the harness-maker at Port Perry, in her snuff-coloured taffeta gown with the bustle and the golden-brown satin trimming, made at home by the visiting dress-maker, on the 'Little Wanzer' sewing-machine; and there was the banker's lady, expertly fitted in the 'tied-back' dress that had been made for her in Toronto or London, in all the modishness of smoked pearl buttons, pleats and bows and laces, dagged edges and chenille fringe. Macdonald met them all. He shook hands with boys in wide-brimmed boater hats, and knickerbockers, and long black stockings, who were led up to him, blushing with embarrassment. He greeted little girls in two-piece taffeta costumes with miniature bows and fringes that were virtually replicas of mamma's. He bent graciously over babies in long elaborately embroidered gowns. He had a word for almost everybody. He knew so many names, remembered so many faces, recalled so many circumstances that usually, in the flashing second of a greeting, the entire form of his interlocutor's existence would miraculously take shape in his mind. He knew the Canadians better than anybody had ever known them before – and better than anybody would ever know them again.

*Donald Creighton*, John A. Macdonald, The Old Chieftain *(Toronto, 1955), p. 221.*

64

*Canadian Illustrated News*

Sir John Addressing a Meeting at Sweetsburgh, Quebec, 1877

# Political Picnics at Napanee and Cobourg

There was a Conservative picnic at Napanee in the following year (1877), and Sir John addressed the crowd from beneath a cedar arch. It was one of a series that was to sweep Macdonald back to power in the election of 1878, after five years in opposition due to the 'Pacific Scandal' in transcontinental railway-building.

In August of the same year another picnic was held at Cobourg, and the Toronto *Mail* describes it in fifteen columns of fine print. A procession of carriages, with two bands, escorted John A. through streets gaily decorated with cedar arches. Old times live again as we read the innumerable streamers and mottos denouncing Liberal policies, announcing Conservative aims, and welcoming Sir John personally.

'Help Our Languishing Industries' is the keynote of the first type. 'The Do-Nothing Policy Is Played Out', says another. 'Trade Languishing', 'Large Deficits', 'Steel Rails Will Rust', and 'Carry the News to Mackenzie' were designed to stress the alleged bad effects of Alexander Mackenzie's administration.

'A National Policy for Canada' was the slogan which more than any other was to bring the Tories back to power in 1878. 'No Compromise – Reciprocity or Protection' referred to trade with the United States. 'The Agricultural and Manufacturing Interests are Hand in Hand', 'Good Times Coming', and 'British Connection' were also prominent banners.

Welcoming Sir John were these: 'Canada's Greatest Statesman', 'See the Conquering Hero Comes!', 'A Thousand Welcomes', 'The Young Men of Cobourg Have Confidence in Sir John', 'The Workingman's Friend', 'We Welcome the Conservative Chief'.

The procession continued with enthusiasm along King Street eastward and south to Boulton's Grove, once owned by the Hon. George S. Boulton in whose law office Sir John had been employed.* The property had passed to his son Colonel D'Arcy E. Boulton, Macdonald's host on this occasion. Speeches occupied most of the afternoon, and in the evening 'a monstrous torchlight procession' half a mile long, headed by the two bands 'and accompanied by a great number of transparencies and a grand display of fireworks', led the crowd to Cobourg's distinguished Victoria Hall where the leader again spoke.

The return to the Boulton residence was something special. The horses of Sir John's carriage were unhitched and he was hauled along by 300 young men with 250 yards of rope. As they passed the four corners at Division Street a balloon ascended; and interspersed with cheers were the strains of 'Auld Lang Syne' and 'Will Ye No Come Back Again'.

*That Macdonald was for a time employed in Boulton's law office in Cobourg is referred to only in Daniel McAllister, *Historical Reminiscences of Cobourg from Its First Settlement* (1903), p. 74. Mr. McAllister died in an accident before completing his account of the town's history. Completion and revision were undertaken by Lieutenant-Colonel Henry Smith of Ottawa and Major George Guillet, ex-M.P., of Cobourg, with the aid of several others long resident in the district. An error relative to Sir John's employment in the Boulton law office is, consequently, hardly conceivable, but he may well have been resident in Cobourg for but a few weeks.

W. S. Herrington, *History of the County of Lennox and Addington*

Sir John at Napanee, 1877

### ANOTHER PUMPKIN GONE!

A MAN was driving a load of pumpkins and squashes up a hill, when a bad boy pulled the tail-board out of his waggon. When he observed the result he stood speechless with rage. "Why don't you swear?" asked another bad boy. "*I have no language equal to the occasion*," replied the unfortunate man.—OLD STORY.

J. W. Bengough, Rapid Grip and Batten Ltd.

# John A. and 'Joe' Rymal

[Joseph Rymal of South Wentworth, one of the wits of the House, often crossed swords with Sir John, both in debate and in repartee. Once in 1882 the subject was the gerrymandering of constituencies – in order 'to hive the Grits' as he put it – and he was very uncomplimentary to Sir John, whose explanations struck him as more fictional than the *Arabian Nights' Entertainment, Sinbad the Sailor,* or *Gulliver's Travels.* The outrage was so great, he said, that even swearing couldn't relieve his feelings.]

I feel [he said] a little like the man addicted to a great deal of profanity, who was driving a waggon-load of pumpkins up a hill. Some of the boys, thinking they would hear some tall swearing, lifted the tail-board out of the waggon. He drove his oxen till he got to the top of the hill, when he looked back and saw the pumpkins rolling down the hill, and the boys waiting to hear what he would say. But he said nothing. One of the boys asked, 'Why don't you swear?' 'Why,' said he, 'I could not do justice to the occasion.'

[Alluding to Tory picnics and speeches during the election campaign of 1878, Joe Rymal said in the House, 'Now, we read of one who went to and fro in the earth, many years ago, and tempted the people by false promises. He tempted our Saviour by taking Him up into a high mountain and showing Him the kingdom of the earth, and promising Him all these if He would fall down and worship him.' Rymal then went on to make the application and to speak of Sir John.]

Sir John: 'But you didn't finish the story about the man who went up into the high mountain.'

Rymal: 'That was not a man, that was the Devil; the other tempter did not go to the top of the mountain; he went round the country holding picnics and tempting the people.' (Laughter.)

Joseph Rymal

[On another occasion, Rymal concluded his remarks about John A. as follows:]

I will suppose that the Hon. First Minister was about to organize his followers into a band of musicians, and were he to ask me what instruments they should play, I would say to him, 'Let everyone play the lyre, because the bandmaster would not have much trouble in making experts of them.'

[For once John A. was annoyed and in no mood for repartee, observing that the tirade showed 'a disposition to scratch and bite' and was derogatory to respect for Parliament.]

69

# Literary Allusions and Quotations

[Before he became an effective speaker John A. was more often in the Legislative Library than on his feet in the House. He read cases and precedents, delved into English classics, and stored his mind with much that was later to be brought forth most appropriately on crucial occasions. In this way he avoided a too-early, inadequate appearance before politicians and lawmakers who could be the most devastating of critics if given the slightest opportunity. His fondness for books was duly noted, and as early as 1846 he was appointed a member of the Library Committee.

Sir John probably made more quotations from English classics than did any other member of the House. During a speech on the budget in 1876 there is an example of pleasant raillery with the addition of an allusion to Shakespeare:]

I heard the threat, the dire threat, that the member for Montreal would go into opposition. . . . I thought I could see a smile, a gentle, placid smile, pass over the countenance of my hon. friend, who knows his power so well. My hon. friend from Montreal is like ancient Pistol – he can speak brave words but, like the same ancient Pistol, he can eat the leek. My hon. friend the Premier was quite satisfied that although the member for Montreal was very brave just now, and although

He casts off his friends
   As huntsman his pack,
For he knows with a word
   He can whistle them back --

they would give him their confidence as they had done hitherto. If the Government are never displaced until through the arm or the accident of my hon. friend from Montreal, they will remain in office much longer than either the wishes of the Opposition or the good of the country require. My hon. friend from Montreal Centre gave me a warning that, unless I accepted this offer at once, there would be no use in throwing my net for him. Well, Mr. Speaker, I have caught some queer fish in my time, but I am afraid my hon. friend is too loose a fish for me to catch.

*Biggar,* Anecdotal Life, *p. 124.*

'The Grand Ministerial Overture, February 13, 1879'

A rare group portrait of Sir John and his cabinet, this cartoon
also recalls 'Joe' Rymal's quip that it would be most fitting if
they all played the lyre.

# A Politician's Memory for Names and Faces

George Guillet, M.P. for West Northumberland in Sir John's day, told me of the great impression the Chief made in his constituency during a campaign of the eighties. 'I introduced him to twenty or thirty farmers in a rural schoolhouse,' he said, 'and after chatting with them for half an hour he called each one by name as he shook hands before continuing on to the next meeting. Not one of these farmers could ever do enough for Sir John thereafter, and they never forgot that they had shaken hands with the Prime Minister.'

When Sir John was touring Ontario and building up political strength while in Opposition as a result of the 'Pacific Scandal' he was at many a political meeting, often both a picnic in the afternoon among farmers and in the evening at the nearest town. Suiting his anecdotes to the occasion, he often told stories with an especial rural flavour. Once in a while, worn out by continual travel and speaking, he had to send substitutes. One farmer, who had come a long distance to be a torchbearer on such an occasion, showed his disappointment by this comment as he threw his torch in the mud: 'I have driven twenty-three miles today over bad roads to carry a torch for John A., and I'll be damned if I carry it for anyone else.'

The personal interest the Chief took in his audience – often going out of his way to shake hands with a political opponent whom he spotted on the edge of a crowd – led to such remarks as, 'Here I have spent all my political life working for Edward Blake, who treats me coldly and haughtily, and along comes Sir John and brings me into his carriage to sit beside him!'

. . . A good friend of mine, who is what we call a Grit, said to me the other day 'What fortunate fellows you are, Macdonald! Here you are with everything prosperous around you, the sun smiles on you, and our fields are teeming with prosperity; while in the days of old, when our own poor friends were in the Government, we had clouded skies and dried-up fields and no crops – and you appropriate all this as your own merits – (laughter) – and the country will be foolish enough to give you credit for what is an act of climate.'

'Sir', said I, 'it only goes to show that Providence is on our side, and if you are a wise man and wish a continuance of the same skies and the same crops you will keep us in power. Be sure, my friend, that the weevil will come again with the Grit.'

Making Sir John a Chief, Council House of the Six Nation Indians near Brantford, Ontario

# Sir John's Reception in Toronto

Sir John arrived at the Nipissing railway station, at the foot of Berkeley street, a few minutes before eight o'clock. Long before that hour, however, crowds of persons anxious to do honour to Canada's greatest statesman, and to show their appreciation of his course in Parliament, assembled in the vicinity of the station. The platform was besieged, the roofs of freight cars in the vicinity were covered with people, and the streets were crowded to an extent which made walking anything but comfortable. On the arrival of the train, Sir John, who was escorted by Mr. J. G. Worts, Mr. W. H. Beatty, and Mr. Denison, was conducted to a carriage amid loud cheers. Having taken his seat the horses were taken from the carriage, and a crowd of willing hands came forward to assist in drawing it and its occupants through the streets. Five hundred torch-bearers were in attendance. . . .

The route of the procession, which lay by way of Berkeley, King, Yonge, Queen, and Simcoe streets, and King street west to the United Empire Club, was lined with people, by whom the greatest enthusiasm was manifested. Along King street during the progress of the demonstration there was one continuous burst of applause, except, perhaps, in the vicinity of the *Globe* office, at which spot cheers were changed to groans, and along Yonge street and Queen street the reception was none the less hearty.

Many of the storekeepers along the route of the procession had illuminated their places of business with an extra display of lamps and gas jets. This was particularly noticeable on Yonge street. The United Empire Club, at which point the procession broke up, was brilliantly illuminated at every window. There, long before the arrival of the procession with Sir John Macdonald, an immense crowd had gathered, and indeed, it was difficult to find room for the passing street cars, and still more difficult to form an avenue towards the Club doors, through which the carriage containing the subject of the demonstration could pass. This was, however, eventually accomplished, and Sir John, amidst much cheering, entered the Club.

*Toronto* Mail, *May 3, 1877.*

*Canadian Illustrated News*

Torchlight Procession in Honour of Sir John, Montreal, 1877

# Grand Tory Demonstration at East York, 1878

The Conservative picnic, which took place at Victoria Park yesterday, will rank as the largest and most influential political gathering ever held in this section of the Dominion. . . . There were about seven thousand persons present. . . . Excursion trains on the Grand Trunk; Northern; Toronto, Grey, and Bruce; and Toronto and Nipissing Railways carried large parties to the Park, while the steamers *Chicora, Picton, Prince Arthur, Norseman, Maxwell, Southern Belle*, and *Watertown* carried thousands to the grounds. The only decoration on the grounds was an arch over the entrance bearing the words 'Welcome to our Chieftain' on one side and 'Protect our Industries' on the other. The pavilion was reserved for ladies, and was crowded by the fair sex during the day. . . . Sir John Macdonald . . . was received with loud cheers. The right honourable gentleman then held a reception of the ladies, several hundred of whom were presented to him. . . . Sir John Macdonald . . . said:

'. . . I am, perhaps, rather fond of the sound of my own voice, and I have been wandering – like the Wandering Jew – from one part of Ontario to the other speaking in this province as well as the Eastern Townships of Quebec. . . . I have to tell you what the old fox-hunter said. This year I have the best lot of dogs that ever I had in my pack. (Laughter.) And they will worry the Grit rat – (renewed laughter) – if you only give them a fair field and no favour. (Applause.) They will not allow themselves to be carried away by a herring drawn across their noses; they will follow the Grit rat – (laughter) – they shall catch the Grit rat, and we will send his skin to Paris to make kid gloves of. (Loud laughter.) Well, gentlemen, we have a great battle before us. . . . I have been, as you know, all my life a Conservative, yet I have been a liberal man. . . . The Grits, you know, are not Reformers; they are hybrids – (laughter) – a cross between a Democrat and an Annexationist. (Hear, hear.) They are neither fish, flesh, nor fowl.'

A voice: 'Nor good red herring.' (Laughter.)

Sir John: 'Nor good red herring, as you say. . . . My opponents may talk about the Pacific Scandal; but Sir Hugh Allan subscribed to the election fund out of his own money, and not out of the public chest. . . . The Grits thought, when they formulated this charge, that they had got me down, and forever – (cries of "never") – but, gentlemen, I was exactly like that child's toy called jack-in-the-box, for as soon as the hands were taken off the lid up popped John A. (Loud laughter.) . . .

*Toronto* Mail, *August 28, 1878.*

Courtesy John R. MacNicol and Harriet Clark

GRAND CONSERVATIVE

# GRAND CONSERVATIVE
# DEMONSTRATION

## VICTORIA PARK

### SCARBORO'

There Will be a Grand

## CONSERVATIVE GATHERING

At Victoria Park, Scarboro', under the auspices of the East York Liberal Conservative Association, on

# TUESDAY, AUGUST 27 1878

From the Electoral Divisions of

| Northumberland, | Toronto, | Hamilton, |
| Durham, | Peel, | Lincoln, |
| Ontario, | Halton, | Welland, |
| York, | Wentworth, | Niagara, |

And Neighbouring Constituencies.

## SIR JOHN MACDONALD

And other leading Men of the party will be present and deliver addresses.

# SPECIAL EXCURSIONS

By boat and rail will be arranged so as to accommodate all these Constituencies.

Full particulars as to the time of leaving the various Ports, Rates of Fare, &c., will be given directly the necessary arrangements are made.   The beautiful grounds the Park are situated within five miles of Toronto, and Steamboats will ply every half hour during the day, between the Park and the City.

JOHN A. MACDONELL,

Secretary of Committee.

# John A.'s Indiscretions

There is an authenticated story of Macdonald in the early sixties. He was Attorney-General for Upper Canada, and lived in lodgings in Quebec. He had been absent from duty for a week; public business was delayed and the Governor-General became impatient. He sent his aide-de-camp, young Lord Bury, to find the absent Minister. Pushing his way past the old house-keeper, Lord Bury penetrated to the bedroom where Macdonald was sitting in bed reading a novel, with a decanter of sherry on the table beside him: 'Mr. Macdonald, the Governor-General told me to say to you that if you don't sober up and get back to business he will not be answerable for the consequences.' Macdonald's countenance reflected the anger he felt at the intrusion: 'Are you here in your official capacity or as a private individual?' 'What difference does that make?' 'Just this,' snapped the statesman, 'If you are here in your official capacity you can go back to Sir Edmund Head, give him my compliments, and tell him to go to hell: if you are simply a private individual you can go yourself!'

*Sir John Willison,* Reminiscences, Political and Personal *(Toronto, 1919), p. 180.*

A similar explosion of great anger occurred in November 1878 while he was at Government House, Halifax, awaiting the arrival of a new governor general, the Marquess of Lorne, and his royal wife the Princess Louise. He was tired from his strenuous duties in Ottawa, and had taken along a supply of brandy. His companions were congenial, and he was soon drinking too much and too often. Even when he reached the lieutenant-governor's house he was hardly presentable, and kept largely to his room. Everyone was embarrassed but himself, but no one liked to disturb him, even though the new governor's ship might dock any minute and all arrangements had been made for his reception. Finally John A.'s secretary was urged to knock at the door and enter. He saw Macdonald in bed, looking more dead than alive and surrounded by a confusion of bottles, documents, newspapers, and books. Apprised of the reason for the interruption, John A. raised himself in bed, surveyed the intruder with hostility, and pointing to the door, said in no uncertain terms: 'Vamoose from this ranch!'

But a few minutes later he pulled himself together and made a reasonably presentable appearance at the reception.

The Landing of the Marquess of Lorne and Princess Louise at Halifax, 1878
*Canadian Illustrated News*

# The National Policy

[Sir John] had been studying the political situation and saw that decay had laid its hand upon the ruling party. The country had fallen into a state of commercial atrophy, and year after year, during the administration of Mr. Mackenzie, saw the situation grow worse. Enterprise was without heart, capital shrank timidly away, and confidence had fairly gone out of the country. . . .

'Our opportunity has come,' said Macdonald to his colleagues at a caucus held about this time. 'Want has overcome the prejudice of a theory, and we will propound a policy that will better this woful state of affairs and carry us back to office.' From that day forth the conservative chief began to organize and marshal his forces, to 'get his hand upon the pulse of the country', and to breathe into his own followers the same hope and ardour that filled himself.

Sir Richard Cartwright [Minister of Finance] jeered at the 'new-fangled doctrines', and his chief [Alexander Mackenzie], losing a momentary restraint upon his vernacular, affirmed in broad Scotch 'that the scheme was the corn laws again with a new face'. The question presented to the ministry was one between commercial misery and a favoured theory, 'but in deference to the formula,' [said Goldwin Smith in *The Bystander*], 'they chose to be stiff-necked, and kicked complaining industry into the camp of their opponents'.

In the House of Commons on the 10th of March, 1876, Sir John boldly laid down the broad 'national policy' of his party in a speech of much vigour and point. His contention was that there should be a thorough reorganization of the tariff, which ought to be constructed in such a manner that it would, while producing sufficient revenue for the current expenses of the country, also afford a stimulus and a protection to home industry, entice capital to the country, and keep our own artisans at home at the employment which must arise under the fostering legislation. Once again the cry went abroad, and at this time at the dictation of the conservative chief: 'Canada for the Canadians!' . . .

On the 17th of September, 1878, the two parties appeared at the polls, Sir Richard Cartwright and the ministry bound neck and heel to their idol; Sir John with the light of hope in his eye and 'Canada for the Canadians!' upon his lips. The change which he predicted had come. It swept the country in a whirlwind and the ministry fell, and their god fell with them:

Like the leaves of the forest when the summer is green,
That host with their banners at sunset were seen;
Like the leaves of the forest when autumn hath blown,
That host on the morrow lay withered and strown.

*G. M. Adam*, Canada's Patriot Statesman: The Life and Career of the Right Honourable Sir John A. Macdonald *(1891), pp. 424-6.*

The Governor General, the Marquess of Lorne, Reading the Speech from the Throne, 1879

# He Assumed No Airs When He Arose to Speak

[In his early political life Macdonald often wore baggy trousers, a long-tailed coat, and a loose necktie. There was a touch of the theatrical in his appearance – his gestures, even his walk had drama, and he had a way of taking his seat much like a bird alighting from flight. This mannerism was accompanied by a quick glance which seemed to take in everything and everybody in a moment – he seemed to comprehend the situation as fully as if he had been present for hours.]

... Mr. Macdonald was as reserved as the staidest veteran in that whole house. He assumed no airs when he arose to speak, and never attempted dramatic or sentimental flights. ... He never spoke merely for the purpose of talking, but only when that which he had to say threw more light upon the discussion, added force to the attack, or strength to the defence. ... 'Sometimes in the thick of the melee,' ... says a gentleman who remembers having seen him there, 'Macdonald was busy in and out of the parliamentary library. I scarce ever remember seeing him then about the house that he was not searching up some case either then impending or to come up at a later date. He was for a great part of his time, too, buried in a study of political and constitutional history.'

*Collins*, Life of Macdonald, *pp. 72-3.*

Apart from the exaggeration that men on the opposite side of the political fence might be expected to use in their stories of John A.'s bad habits, there are always people who feel that by depreciating the famous they somehow add to their own meagre stock of virtue. Tales of the drinking habits of great men die hard. Some, like Sir Winston Churchill, encouraged such stories, or at least did not discourage them.

Thomas D'Arcy McGee, noted as an orator, was also known to be a heavy drinker. When some of the party protested to Sir John he took an opportunity to speak to McGee: 'Look here, McGee, this Government cannot afford two drunkards, and you've got to stop!'

Gentlemen, I feel bound to follow the example set me by the Premier of Canada – by the Hon. Alexander Mackenzie – for we must be careful to speak of him as the Hon. Alexander Mackenzie in the future. (Laughter.) We all got a lesson lately, which I know you will take to heart, in politeness and deportment. We were told that no more must he be styled Sandy Mackenzie (Renewed laughter): that no more must such a one be spoken of as Archie McKellar, or another as Geordie Brown; that you must speak of them as the Honourable Archibald McKellar and the Honourable George Brown. I didn't know, gentlemen, before I read that speech, what a deeply injured man I was myself; I didn't know that the people of Canada, from the Atlantic to the Pacific, had been insulting me for thirty years by calling me 'John A.' (Laughter and cheers.)

*Banquet to Thomas White, Montreal, November 24, 1875.* Liberal Conservative Hand-Book, Grits in Office, 1876, *p. 4.*

# Quips and Aphorisms

'They say lawyers make the best of soldiers because they are so ready for the charge.'

'An election is like a horse-race, in that you can tell more about it the next day.'

'Given a government with a big surplus, a big majority, and a weak opposition, you could debauch a committee of archangels.'

To John Carling: 'John, I wonder if God Almighty ever made a man as honest as you look?'

'A compliment is the statement of an agreeable truth; flattery is the statement of an agreeable untruth.'

'Let's not quarrel about the skin until we kill the bear.'

Of a Scotch Liberal in Parliament: 'He is Mackenzie and water.'

Of a brilliant but erratic M.P.: 'The world would never have heard of him if God Almighty had given him common sense.'

Watching female acrobats at the Provincial Exhibition in Kingston: 'No doubt it is a custom to show the calves first.'

'It's devilish hard for a free trader to make a Protectionist speech' – a remark which his political opponents said arose from his own experience.

Mr. Holton: 'I have the floor; the right hon. gentleman has made a statement in a menacing manner, pointing his finger at me, and I call upon him to explain the meaning of it.'
Sir John: 'All I can say is, if I pointed my finger at the hon. gentleman, I take my finger back.'

[One of Sir John's most famous remarks was repeated in various forms when men who usually supported him broke away on minor details of the Confederation issue or other causes, great or small. Senator Dickey of Nova Scotia, a delegate at the first conference on Confederation, was one of these, opposing Nova Scotia's entry on the ground that an insufficient subsidy was being granted that province. He did not get an appointment as Lieutenant-Governor of Nova Scotia, for which his name had been mentioned. Soon afterwards, Sir John met him and this conversation ensued:]
Sir John: 'Why did you kick up your heels on the Confederation question? Have you gone over to the enemy?'
Senator Dickey: 'No, I am still a Conservative, and I shall support you whenever I think you are right.'
Sir John: 'That is no satisfaction.' There was a twinkle in his eye as he continued, 'Anybody may support me when I am right. What I want is a man who will support me when I am wrong!'

Mr. Mackenzie (commenting on a clause in a new bill): 'If that is considered an improvement, it is certainly one of a Tory character.'
Sir John: 'A satisfac-Tory character.'

The Great Conservative Banquet at Ottawa, 1879

# The Canadian Pacific Railway

[The 'Pacific Scandal' having effectively delayed for most of a decade the construction of the Canadian Pacific Railway – for the administration of Alexander Mackenzie had no vision beyond linking waterways by rail – Sir John had almost to begin anew on the project. On January 17, 1881, he made a notable speech in the House on conflicting attitudes adopted by the Opposition.]

Sir John: ... The pledges made to British Columbia and the pledges made in reference to the future of this Dominion will be carried out under the auspices of a Conservative Government and with the support of a Conservative majority. (Applause.) ... We have had tragedy, comedy, and farce from the other side. (Laughter and applause.) Sir, it commenced with tragedy (hear, hear); the contract was declared oppressive; the amount of money to be given was enormous; we were giving away the whole lands of the North-West; not an acre was to be left for the free and independent foot of the free and independent settler; there was to be a monopoly handed over to this company. ... This was the tragedy (hear, hear), and the honourable gentlemen opposite played it so well that if they did not affect the whole audience, we could see tears of pity trickling down the cheeks of gentlemen sitting on that side of the House. (Laughter.) Then, sir, we had the comedy. The comedy was that when every one of the speeches of these honourable gentlemen was read to them, it was proved last year, or the year before, and in previous years, they had thought one way, and that now they spoke in another way. (Hear, hear.) This was the most amusing and comical thing in the world. Every honourable gentleman got up and said, 'I am not bound by that (hear, hear); it is true that I said so two years ago, but circumstances are changed in two years (or one year, or in eight months in one case), but to what I said eight months ago I am not bound now.' (Cheers and laughter.) This was very comic (laughter); it amused us all; it amused the House, and the whole country chuckled on a broad grin. (Laughter.) These honourable gentlemen said it was true we were fools eight months ago ...

The policy of the leader of the Opposition ... would be to stop all work in British Columbia; not a mile would be built, not a train would ever run through British Columbia if he could help it. ... Yes, I am proud to say that if our scheme is carried out, the steamer landing in Halifax will discharge its freight and emigrants upon a British railway, which will go through Quebec and through Ontario to the far west on British territory, under the British flag, under Canadian laws, and without any chance of either the immigrant being deluded or seduced in any way from his allegiance or his proposed residence in Canada, or the traffic coming from England or from Asia being subjected to the possible prohibition or offensive restrictive taxation or customs regulations of a foreign power.

House of Commons Debates *(1881), Vol. X, p. 485 ff.*

H.

*Canadian Illustrated News*

'Pacific Railway Falconry'

Johnny Macdonald: Yon's no the way to train a bird, mon. If ye dinna tak care he'll fly awa'.

Sandy Mackenzie: Indeed that's just what I'm wishing the noo.

# The Donkey Had a Vote

John A. did not believe in universal suffrage, and considered that no one who did had a right to call himself a Conservative. Once when he was talking on the matter in the House a member interrupted to ask a question. 'Certainly,' said Sir John. 'Well,' said the member, 'many years ago, during the gold fever, I went out to California, and while there working in the diggings I acquired an interest in a donkey. Under it I voted. Before the next election came round the donkey died, and then I had no vote. . . . Who voted on the first election, I or the donkey?' It was on the tip of his tongue to retort it didn't much matter which, but Sir John merely joined in the general laughter. If women had the property qualification he was in favour of their having the right to vote. He said in an address in Cobourg in 1886 that he would do his utmost to obtain the franchise for them, but nothing further came of it. He told Joseph Pope, his secretary, that he believed women were largely conservative in their views, and would 'strengthen the bulwarks against unbridled democracy'.

When driving with his secretary to Goldwin Smith's Toronto home, 'The Grange', in 1887, Sir John asked him if he had ever been there before. He hadn't. 'Well,' said Sir John, 'you are going to a very interesting house with a charming host, but notice Mr. Smith's habit of interlarding his otherwise agreeable conversation with tiresome references to the nobility. Why, to hear him talk, you would imagine he never consorted in England with anybody under the rank of an earl.' Later, on the way to the train, 'Did you observe what I told you? That's why Dizzy in *Lothair* called him a social parasite. Strange that so brilliant a man, who needs no adventitious aids, should manifest such a weakness.' Macdonald and Smith had but little in common. But once in the Queen's Hotel, Toronto, he said to Smith: 'My dear sir, I forgive you everything for your splendid defence of the Empire.' Sixteen years after John A.'s death Goldwin Smith said of him that 'if he was partisan he was not opportunist'.

In the preamble to the Jesuit Estates Act were many ostentatious references to the Pope and the Church that most Protestants of the day considered highly objectionable, but the Act was wholly within Quebec's rights as a province and therefore not disallowed. Sir John thought these obnoxious phrases were inserted to tempt him into error, which would have been disastrous to his position particularly in Quebec, Ontario, and Manitoba. In 1888 Honoré Mercier, a Liberal M.P. from Quebec, tried to pump him as to his attitude towards the Act, and finally asked him directly. Sir John replied: 'Do you take me for a damn fool?'

J. W. Bengough, Rapid Grip and Batten Ltd.

'The Great Political Conjurer'

'All sorts of wine poured out of one and the same bottle.'

# You'll Never Die, John A.!

[At a demonstration in Toronto to celebrate Sir John's forty years in Parliament, December 17, 1884, the guest of honour said:]

. . . This is not only a great and glorious incident but it is also a very solemn one. When I look back through my forty years of public life; when I remember how few remain of those who with me entered full of hope, life, and the earnestness of youth; when I bear in mind that those who do remain are like myself, feeble old men – (cries of 'No, no!' and a voice, 'You'll never die, John A.!') – when I think of all this, feelings of a most solemn nature awake in my mind. . . . I heard a cry just now from one of my friends saying 'You will never die!' (Laughter.) Gentlemen, I really do believe that those who are in political opposition to me think so too – (renewed laughter) – and I fear, though they pray for me and all other like sinners, that in the supplications there is no pious expression of the desire that my life may be long spared. (Loud laughter.) They have no objection that I should go to another and a better world, and that I should not prolong my stay in this one. (Loud laughter.) I am happy, gentlemen, to state to you that your good wishes with respect to the renewal and the continuance of my health have been to a very great extent realized. (Loud cheering.) Thanks to a good conscience and to Sir Andrew Clark I come back to you nearly as good as new – (cheers and laughter) – a little the worse for wear, to be sure – (laughter) – but still able to stand the battle for a few years longer. (Cheers.) I was much amused, gentlemen, when in England to read a sentence in a Toronto newspaper, stating that the position of the Opposition was simply this: 'If Sir John A.'s stomach gives in, then the Opposition will go in – (loud laughter) – but if John A.'s stomach holds out, then we will stay out.' (Continued laughter.) You will be glad to know that there are strong indications that they will stay out. (Hear, hear!)

*"Hail to the Chief!", Toronto* Mail, *December 18, 1884.*

'Another Mile-Stone Passes; or, Father Time as Spry as Ever'

J. W. Bengough, Rapid Grip and Batten Ltd.

J. W. Bengough, Rapid Grip and Batten Ltd.

'Good News from 'Ome!'

Dr. Andrew Clark: You only require rest, sir; you are not suffering from any organic trouble.

Sir John (aside to G.B.): Wonder how *he* found out that the *Globe* is not an organ.

Sir John, who was loudly applauded, commenced by making some jocular references to the Globe's statement that he was insane. It said a Cabinet Minister had to go round with him to take care of him, but as there was no Cabinet Minister present on that occasion he (Sir John) must have escaped from his keeper. (Laughter.) He had been charged with committing all the crimes in the calendar. It was said in 1873 that he had committed suicide by jumping off the wharf at Rivière du Loup – (laughter) – that his constitution was a hopeless wreck, that he had cancer in the stomach and paralysis of the brain – (renewed laughter) – and now they charged him with being a hopeless imbecile, and not allowed to walk alone. (Laughter.) Well, as he was enjoying a few lucid moments just then – (laughter) – before a fit of frenzy came on – (renewed laughter) – he would discuss some of the questions of the day.

*Toronto* Mail, *February 12, 1887.*

91

# The Macdonalds at Home

In private life Sir John has his circle of warm admirers as well as at the public board. He is frank and genial by temperament, kind and courteous in his social relations – 'a very prince', says a distinguished guest once at his house, and a warm admirer, 'at his own board'. That winning grace of manner, which those who do not know him think he wears for political purposes in public life, shines out still more brightly in the domestic and social sphere; that it is really impossible to know Sir John at the fireside or the board and not to love him. . . . Mr. Goldwin Smith . . . tells us . . . 'of a statesman who knows how to lay politics aside in the social hour and is large-minded enough to bear with opinions differing from his own'.

But the crown to Sir John's social success is given by the place his very accomplished and popular wife Lady Macdonald fills at the capital. Of the society circle there she is voted pre-eminently the queen; where in every project of social enterprise she is the first and the last, and no less the favourite of the elderly and the demure than of the young folk. . . . In political questions too this gifted lady takes no little interest, and her judgment is said to be scarce less sound than that of Sir John, who, it is whispered, is in the habit of consulting her when he is about to take some important political step. . . .

In domestic life Lady Macdonald is a model woman, lavishing her tenderness upon an invalid daughter, keeping a household that might well be the envy of any circle; attending to Sir John at late sittings of the House and, as Mrs. Disraeli used to do, and as Mrs. Gladstone does, wrapping up her husband after he has made a speech, and zealously guarding his health at home or while travelling. . . . When not receiving friends at dinner, or in some other social way, Sir John is to be found in his little library attending to public business or reading until very late at night.

*Collins,* Life of Macdonald, *pp. 505-8.*

*The Dominion Illustrated*

'Earnscliffe'

Formerly known as Reynolds' house, it was purchased by Sir John in 1883.
He gave it the name, which means 'the eagle's cliff'.

# Sir John Honoured in England

A dinner in honour of Sir John A. Macdonald, Prime Minister of Canada, was given at the Empire Club, Grafton-street, last night. The Marquis of Lorne presided. He was supported, among others, by the Duke of Sutherland, Viscount Bury, the Earl of Kimberley, [and many others].

The Chairman, in proposing the toast of 'Sir John Macdonald', expressed the gratification it gave him to propose the health and prosperity of one who was the most successful statesman of what was the most successful among the younger nations of the world. . . .

The Marquis of Salisbury . . . hoped that Canada might fully attain to the high prospect which her destiny seemed to point to, and that in many a future year she might look back with pride to the infancy which had been nurtured by the care of England, and which owed so much to the superintending sagacity and wisdom of statesmen like their distinguished guest. (Cheers.) He could wish Canada no better wish than that in the long future she might have many statesmen to shed as much lustre on her history and confer as many benefits on her people as Sir John Macdonald. (Cheers.) . . .

Sir John Macdonald, who was cordially received, said it had been a special gratification to him to have his health proposed by the chairman, under whom he had served five or six years, during which the noble marquis had governed wisely and well and to the acceptance of the people of Canada. (Cheers.) . . . After referring to the great progress which Canada had made since he entered public life in that country 40 years ago, he said that the majority of the people of Canada, apart from a sentiment of loyalty, had a well-grounded opinion that the best interests of the country, political, moral, and material, were involved in a continuous connexion with the mother country. (Cheers.) . . . He believed that the tie between the dependencies and the mother country was so strong that if no federation existed Canada would still remain a portion of the British Empire of her own choice. . . . Arrangements should be made for a closer commercial alliance, and, above all, for a common system of defence and offence. (Cheers.)

The Times *(London), November 27, 1884.*

Public Archives of Canada

# Sir John Has His Head 'Read'

This gentleman has a remarkably sharp and active organization. The mental temperament predominates, which gives him quickness, clearness, and intensity of mind. He has also a full degree of the motive temperament which gives a wiry toughness and strength of organization, elasticity of action, and a good degree of endurance, which sustains him in the mental labours induced by his highly wrought nervous temperament.

There is a great prominence of the lower portion of the forehead, indicating large perceptive organs which give a quick, ready, and clear perception of facts, things, business, and whatever comes within the range of practical life and effort. This is essentially an intelligent forehead. He is strongly endowed with order which renders him methodical and systematic in whatever he does. His language, which is indicated by the fullness and prominence of the eye, indicates uncommon power of speech, ability to talk with ease, clearness, and copiousness, and also to remember everything he reads. His locality would enable him to remember the place on a page where a fact was recorded. His large eventuality renders him capable of retaining the history and the incidents which form a part of his experience or of that which he gathers from reading.

The upper part of his forehead is not as large. He is not so much a philosopher as he is a practical man. He has to do with facts and their bearing on common life. He is fond of wit and amusement, must be excellent in conversation, and at home in the social circle. He has respect for whatever is venerable. The organs which give firmness, pride, ambition, and energy are also strongly developed, but are not distinctly seen.

Such persons need an abundance of sleep, temperate habits, much exercise in the open air, and relaxation of mind and cultivation of bodily vigour, otherwise they break down early because they overdo and exhaust their vitality prematurely.

American Phrenological Journal, *quoted in Macpherson*, Life of Macdonald, *I, 394-5.*

John A. seldom missed an opportunity to relieve the tedium of parliament with a quip. On the appointment of a Fisheries Committee he said that he was expecting a good report, 'for there is both a Fisher and an Anglin on the committee'.

'Phrenological Chart of the Head of the Country'

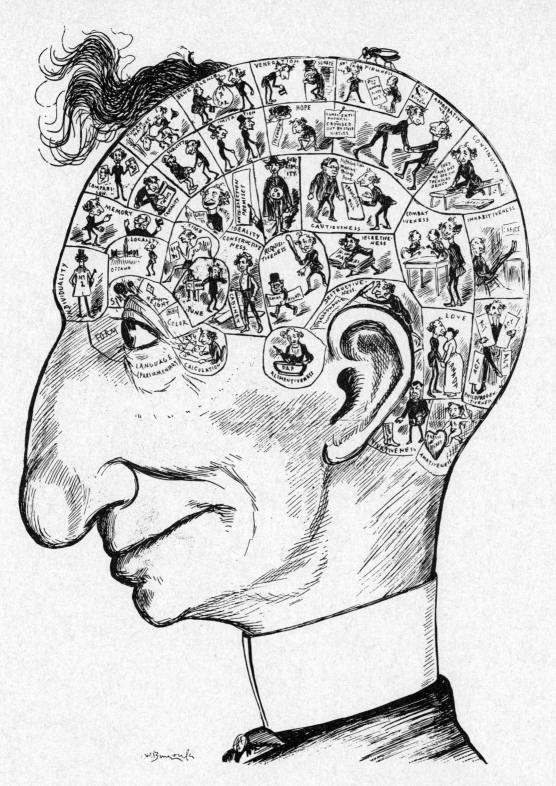

J. W. Bengough, Public Archives of Canada

A RIEL UGLY POSITION.

J. W. Bengough, Rapid Grip and Batten Ltd.

# The Execution of Louis Riel

Sir Hector Langevin [Minister of Public Works]: '... The sentence of death was the sentence of the law.... [Riel] had attacked the authority of the Queen; ... he had called the half-breeds to his aid ... ; he had destroyed their religion to establish one of his own, and my friends from the Province of Quebec call that man a compatriot, a man of their race! No, Mr. Speaker; the sober second thought of the people will not be so.... We found ... to our great regret, that we could not interfere.... I hope this House will remember that we did only our duty in the matter, and, though we did it reluctantly, we did it. We do not deny that we did it; we say boldly that we did it....'

Mr. Laurier: '... Sir, in the Province to which I belong, and especially among the race to which I belong, the execution of Louis Riel has been universally condemned as being the sacrifice of a life, not to inexorable justice, but to bitter passion and revenge.... But that he was insane seems to me beyond the possibility of controversy, ... and I repeat again that we cannot make a nation of this new country by shedding blood, but by extending mercy and charity for all political offences.'

Sir Adolphe Caron [Minister of Militia and Defence]: '... I do not wish, Sir, to be misunderstood. I felt, and I feel to-day, more than I can express, how painful was the duty which we were called upon to perform. I felt that it was not a light thing to sever those ties, political and social, which had bound me to those friends and countrymen who had entrusted me with their confidence and who withdrew it on that occasion. But I felt that it was my imperative duty to my own Province of Quebec, which I love so much, to take the course I did.... It is necessary for us to show that, whether in the extreme North-West or in the older Provinces, the Government of Canada is sufficiently strong to protect her people and to maintain law and order.... Under those circumstances we felt that it was of the utmost necessity that we should allow the law of the land to take its course in the case of Louis Riel....'

House of Commons Debates, *1886, XXI, pp. 73-358.*

[As almost all political decisions are, the Riel controversy was decided on a careful estimate of the expediency of the courses open. Macdonald, who took no part in the debate, had no sympathy for Riel, but the gains and losses in voting strength and political loyalties of the two racial groups were carefully canvassed before final action was taken. The Quebec election of 1886 was fought largely on the issue, and was won by Honoré Mercier and his 'nationalists' in opposition to the Macdonald policy, but in the Federal election of 1887 the Conservatives retained a sufficient number of Quebec seats to remain in power. In the long run, however, the party was destined to lose Quebec's support, which went to the Liberals under Laurier.]

# The Darling Dream of His Heart

[Sir John and Lady Macdonald finally set out on their transcontinental journey over the Canadian Pacific Railway in July, 1886. The time of departure from Ottawa was kept secret, and there was no public send-off. Some travel inconveniences were avoided, for the private car *Jamaica* had been thoughtfully fitted with window screens of fine mesh to protect them from flies and dust. Fortunately Lady Macdonald wrote an intimate account of their thoughts and experiences.]

Before we reach Port Arthur, where business begins, I must introduce some of our travelling party. Our 'Chief' – who among many other offices holds that of Superintendent-General of Indian affairs – I shall sometimes call by the translation of an Indian name given him by Crowfoot, Chief of the Blackfeet, *Kis-ta-mo-ni-mon*, or 'Our Brother-in-law'. First then comes 'Our Brother-in-law', a very well known personage in Canada, who is taking this special trip for a 'special' purpose. He has come to see the realization of the darling dream of his heart, – a railway from ocean to ocean, the development of many million acres of magnificent country, and the birth of a new nation.

During seventeen years, in and out of Parliament, he had battled for these changes, through discouragement, obloquy, and reverse, and with a strong patience all his own had bided his time until as years went on, men, resolute like himself, had arisen to take the aid his Government were determined to offer for the development of this vast territory by the completion of this railway. During the forty years and in the various capacities he had tried, in his poor way, faithfully to serve Queen and country, no happier hours had come to him, I think, than these, as he sits thoughtful in the *Jamaica*, looking on the varied scenes through which we pass.

*Lady Macdonald, 'By Car and By Cowcatcher',* Murray's Magazine, *London, 1887, pp. 222-3.*

At Winnipeg they were guests of Lieutenant-Governor Aikins for three days, with receptions and a public meeting at the Royal Roller Rink where John A. expressed his satisfaction at living long enough to travel over the railway from coast to coast, rather than, as some friends had suggested, 'from the serene heights of heaven above', or, as his enemies assumed, 'from the pit beneath.' 'I have now', he quipped, 'disappointed both friends and foes, and am taking a horizontal view.'

Sir John and Lady Macdonald at Port Arthur, 1886

# By Car and By Cowcatcher

[Lady Agnes Macdonald rode in 'the car of the engine' between Calgary and Loggan, and saw everything with ease, though 'the Chief', as well as the engineer, were not too pleased to have her there. Her next move was to the cowcatcher of the engine, where she kept her position even through tunnels at 50 miles per hour, with water from springs dripping on her from the roof.]

The Chief, seated on a low chair on the rear platform of the car, with a rug over his knees and a magazine in his hand, looked very comfortable and content. Hearing my request, after a moment's thought he pronounced the idea 'rather ridiculous', then remembered it was dangerous as well, and finally asked if I was sure I could hold on. Before the words were well out of his lips, and taking permission for granted by the question, I was again standing by the cowcatcher, admiring the position of the candle-box, and anxiously asking to be helped on.

Before I take my seat, let me try, briefly, to describe the 'cowcatcher'. Of course every one knows that the buffer-beam is that narrow, heavy iron platform, with the sides scooped out, as it were, on the very fore-front of the engine over which the headlight glares, and in the corner of which a little flag is generally placed. In English engines, I believe, the buffers proper project from the front of this beam. In Canadian engines another sort of attachment is arranged, immediately below the beam, by which the engine can draw trains backwards as well as forwards. The beam is about eight feet across at the widest part, and about three feet deep. The description of a cowcatcher is less easy. To begin with, it is misnamed, for it catches no cows at all. Sometimes, I understand, it throws up on the buffer-beam whatever maimed or mangled animal it has struck, but in most cases it clears the line by shoving forward, or tossing aside, any removable obstruction. It is best described as a sort of barred iron beak, about six feet long, projecting close over the track in a V shape, and attached to the buffer-beam by very strong bolts. It is sometimes sheathed with thin iron plates in winter, and acts then as a small snowplough.

Behold me now, enthroned on the candle-box, with a soft felt hat well over my eyes, and a linen carriage-cover tucked round me from waist to foot. Mr. E—— had seated himself on the other side of the headlight. He had succumbed to the inevitable, ceased further expostulation, disclaimed all responsibility, and, like the jewel of a Superintendent he was, had decided on sharing my peril! I turn to him, peeping round the headlight with my best smile. 'This is *lovely*,' I triumphantly announce, seeing that a word of comfort is necessary, '*quite lovely*; I shall travel on this cowcatcher from summit to sea.'

Lady Agnes Macdonald
Photo by H. D. Topley, Public Archives of Canada

*Lady Macdonald*, Murray's Magazine.

# Sir John Rides the Cowcatcher

[At Palliser] the Chief and his friends walked up to the cowcatcher to make a morning call. I felt a little 'superior' and was rather condescending. Somewhat flushed with excitement but still anxious to be polite, I asked 'would the Chief step up and take a drive?' To the horror of the bystanders he carelessly consented, and in another moment had taken the place of Mr. E——, the latter seating himself at our feet on the buffer-beam. There was a general consternation among our little groups of friends and the few inhabitants of Palliser – the Chief 'rushing through the flats of the Columbia on a cowcatcher'. . . . Everyone was horrified. It is a comfort to the other occupant of the buffer to find some one else wilful, and as we steamed away towards Donald, at the eastern base of the Selkirks, I felt not so bad after all!

*Lady Macdonald*, Murray's Magazine.

When Sir John alighted from the train at Regina during his trip, he saw a dead level plain extending in all directions as far as the eye could reach. One of those who welcomed him on the station platform asked him somewhat gushingly what he thought of the prospect. With a twinkle in his eye, and his noted quiet smile, he said: 'If you had a little more wood, a little more water, and here and there a hill, I think the prospect would be improved.'

At a reception during the journey, a Belgian bishop expressed surprise at the appearance of an escort in Highland costume. He asked Sir John why the men were without trousers.

Sir John: 'It is merely a local custom. In some places people take off their hats as a mark of honour to distinguished guests; here they take off their trousers.'

The train reached Port Moody on Saturday morning, July 24, and the steamer *Princess Anne* carried the Prime Minister and his party to Victoria. Reporting the occasion, the press observed that Sir John 'looks as gay as a lark'.

Sir John Crossing Rogers Pass
Jefferys accompanied the party as a reporter for the Toronto *Mail*.
C. W. Jefferys, Canadian Pacific Railway Company

# Reception at New Westminster

At a public meeting on Thursday night the people decided unanimously that the veteran statesman should have a right Royal reception, and that the expenses be paid out of the city exchequer. It was also resolved to make application for a gunboat to aid in giving a salute.

On Friday morning at 10 o'clock the Mayor and Council met in the Council Chambers and proceeded to make arrangements in accordance with the expressed wishes of the people. The Mayor and Council, with other representative men, will form the reception committee. Several committees have been appointed to take charge of decorations and processions on land and water and the preservation of order. The great statesman will be escorted by the reception committee, and by citizens in carriages, to the parlour of the old government house, which will be fitted up and decorated: and there he will be received by two or three distinguished citizens and the ladies. The people will be waiting for him on the grass in front of the house, and there will be markees, tents, and music. The whole affair will be a well arranged impromptu reception, or a pic-nic on a grand scale. If we may judge of a coming event by the shadow, it is certain Sir John will get a *cead mile a faithe* and find himself 'AT HOME' in the Royal City.

*New Westminster* Mainland Guardian, *July 24, 1886.*

The Reception for Sir John and Lady Macdonald at Government House, New Westminster, 1886

# John A. as a Ladies' Man

[A meeting in Cobourg early in December of 1886 exemplifies political gatherings – sometimes two or three a day – where no great speeches were given but people were put in a good humour. The railway car *Jamaica,* in which Sir John had made his western trip over the C.P.R. in the summer of 1886, was also at his disposal later that year, and accompanied by three cabinet ministers – the Hon. J. S. D. Thompson, the Hon. George Foster, and the Hon. Thomas White – he was at Cobourg early in December in the interest of the re-election of George Guillet, M.P. for West Northumberland. Sir John went out of his way on this occasion to address the youth of Victoria College, then in Cobourg, and to flatter the ladies.]

'I thank the young gentlemen connected with Victoria University for presenting me with this beautiful address. . . . Some of them, I think, were wishing they were a little older, as I saw the feeling of envy on their faces when, taking the privilege of age, I snatched a pretty kiss from the young lady who presented me with a bouquet. (Roars of laughter.) . . . I also thank the ladies of Cobourg for their beautiful floral gift. When I get home my wife will probably ask how I came to get the gift, and I will tell her it was because I promised, as I do promise you, to do my utmost to get the ladies the right to vote. (Applause and laughter.) The Liberal-Conservative party is the party of union. (Much laughter.) No doubt some of you are looking around among the undergraduates and thinking, believing, and rejoicing that they too belong to the party of union.' (Renewed laughter.) As he sat down, someone called out 'What's the matter with John A.?' And the students and the crowd roared out 'He's all right! He's all right!' Five hundred torch-bearers and a band then escorted Sir John to his carriage.

*Toronto* Mail, *December 4 and 6, 1886.*

In August-September of 1890 Sir John made a trip by steamship to the Maritimes. While on the St. John River he was informed that a stop would be made at Gagetown and was asked if he would speak there. 'I can't tell,' he said, 'until I see the crowd.' When they arrived he made one of his pleasant little speeches from the deck of the steamer. At the next stop he gave no address but went ashore among those who had gathered, patting children, kissing babies, giving a flower to a little girl, and being pleasant to numerous elderly people. When he returned to the ship someone asked him why he spoke at one place and did not at the other. 'Why, they were mostly men at Gagetown,' he said, 'but here nearly all were women and children.'

Public Archives of Canada

109

# We Are All British Subjects

Wilfrid Laurier: '. . . We ought to remember this – French, English, Liberals, Conservatives – that no race in this country has absolute rights, only the rights which do not invade the rights of any other race. We ought to remember that the expression of race feelings and race sentiments should be well restrained to a point, beyond which, if pressed, though still kept within legitimate limits, they might hurt the feelings and sentiments of other races. . . .'

Sir John A. Macdonald: 'I have no accord with the desire expressed in some quarters that by any mode whatever there should be an attempt made to oppress the one language or to render it inferior to the other; I believe that would be impossible if it were tried, and it would be foolish and wicked if it were possible. . . . There is no paramount race in this country; there is no conquered race in this country; we are all British subjects. . . . Again and again have we been put in a minority because we declined to join in that crusade against the French Canadians, against the Catholic religion, and against French institutions. Again and again have I been misrepresented and called the slave of popery, and told that I had sold myself to the French of Lower Canada and was sacrificing my own race, my own religion, and my own people because, without a moment of hesitation, without swerving for an instant, I and those who followed me – for even when I was not the nominal leader, I greatly directed the course of the Conservative Party – declined, from no personal motive or desire of popularity – the popular cry was raised against the French Canadians in Upper Canada then as it is in Ontario to-day – to do an injustice to our French-Canadian fellow-citizens.'

House of Commons Debates, *February 17, 1890.*

Sir John, replying in 1889 to Mr. Laurier's statement that his (Laurier's) followers were small in number, said 'Why are they a small body? Because the country does not give them the same confidence it does us. The hon. gentleman knows that under the dome of St. Paul's in London, there is a celebrated epitaph to Sir Christopher Wren: *Si monumentum requiris, circumspice* – if you seek for a monument look around you! We say the same thing in a humble spirit. Look around at the prosperity of the country; look at the undiminished confidence which the people have in us from one end of the country to another. That is our best monument, and I expect by-and-by to see something of that kind inscribed on my tombstone.'

Mr. Paterson (Brant): 'Will you see your own tombstone?'

Sir John: 'I will be looking down on my tombstone. I will be looking down on the Conservative majority, which I shall leave in such good spirit that they will carry on the traditions that have guided them since 1854.'

House of Commons Debates, *1889.*

Wilfrid Laurier, 1890
Public Archives of Canada

# Sir John on Canadian Unity

If I had influence over the minds of the people of Canada, any power over their intellect, I would leave them this legacy: 'Whatever you do, adhere to the Union. We are a great country, and shall become one of the greatest in the universe if we preserve it; we shall sink into insignificance and adversity if we suffer it to be broken.' God and nature made the two Canadas one – let no factious men be allowed to put them asunder.

.    .    .

The statement that has been made so often that this is a conquered country is *à propos de rien*. Whether it was conquered or ceded, we have a constitution now under which all British subjects are in a position of absolute equality having equal rights of every kind – of language, of religion, of property, and of person. There is no paramount race in this country; we are all British subjects, and those who are not English are none the less British subjects on that account.

House of Commons Debates, *February 17, 1890*.

The truth is you British Canadians never can forget that you were once supreme. . . . No man in his senses can suppose that the country can for a century to come be governed by a totally unfrenchified government. If a British Canadian desires to conquer, he must 'stoop to conquer'. He must make friends of the French without sacrificing the status of his race or religion. He must respect their nationality. Treat them as a nation and they will act as a free people generally do – call them a faction and they become factious.

*John A. to Brown Chamberlin, June 21, 1856.*

THE OLD FLAG,
THE OLD POLICY,
THE OLD LEADER.

# John A., Raconteur

The most select but least pretentious public-bar in Canada [observed Samuel P. Day in *English America, or Pictures of Canadian Places and People* in 1864] is 'Dolly's' in Montreal. The proprietor is an Englishman who has resided some thirty or forty years in our dependency and whose personal appearance is as singular as his eccentricities are remarkable. Here officers of the Guards, judges, and some of the leading gentlemen of the city daily congregate. Conversation is indulged, and sometimes when a party of friends happen to meet, various interesting stories are told connected with the colony.

[Members of Parliament were habitués of Dolly's in the period when Montreal was the seat of government and John A. was Receiver General. He came in with a crowd one day and began to entertain them with stories. Tea was served, the evening wore on, and, says E. B. Biggar, the round of stories continued until daylight, with a fish breakfast served gratis by the proprietor – for a good deal had been spent on drinks. The biggest fish of all was placed in front of the greatest story-teller, and there was no doubt who that was.]

Once, when he had been over-drinking, John A. was about to follow a Grit speaker who had outlined his party's platform. He was sick at his stomach just as he was about to commence. The day seemed lost, but he was equal to the occasion. 'That's always the way the Grit policy affects me. It just makes me sick!'

[During discussion of a bill of 1877 relative to crime and punishment, a member suggested that it reminded him of the old blue laws of Connecticut.] 'If the Minister of Justice [Mr. Blake] will not consent to more amendments (he continued) I will move the six months' hoist.'

Mr. Blake: 'The hon. gentleman has not yet convinced me. I am open to conviction.'

Sir John: 'A good many persons will be open to conviction under the bill.'

A Member [speaking on the question of maintaining order among the Indians in the Northwest]: 'A small party of troops going through a mountain-pass was unexpectedly attacked by Indians. The emergency was great; they had not time to dismount the howitzers, but pointed them and fired from the backs of the mules, creating great consternation among the Indians.'

Sir John: 'And among the mules!'

J. W. Bengough, Rapid Grip and Batten Ltd.

# Disraeli and Macdonald Compared

Sir John Macdonald is a type of politician which has never failed to delight the English people – the man who, like Palmerston, can work hard, do strong things, hold his purpose, never lose sight for a moment of the honour and welfare of his country, and yet crack his joke and have his laugh, full of courage and good spirits and kindly fun. . . . Sir John Macdonald in the English House of Commons would have been equal, in my opinion, to Mr. Disraeli in finesse in the art of forming combinations and managing men. He never could have equalled him in invective, or in epigram, or in force as an orator. Sir John Macdonald brings up his artillery with more ease. He is always human, even in his attacks. Lord Beaconsfield, as Mr. Disraeli in the House of Commons, approached his opponent like some serpentine monster, coiled himself ruthlessly round him, fascinated with his gaze, and struck out with venomed fang. But Sir John is probably the better debater of the two. His delivery is lively, natural, mercurial; Lord Beaconsfield's is labored. The power of making a statement is not the forte of the author of *Endymion*. Sir John Macdonald makes a luminous statement, and his reasoning faculty is at least as high as

Lord Beaconsfield's. He has very little comparatively, of the latter's *curiosa felicitas* in coining phrases, but his humour is more spontaneous. Lord Beaconsfield has the charm which is inseparable from genius, but it may well be doubted if his power of conciliating men and fixing their affections surpasses that of the Prime Minister of the Dominion. I am sure that in sober strong sense the balance is in favour of the Canadian statesman. There is nothing viewy about Sir John Macdonald. Though a man of imagination, reason is lord every time.

*N. F. Davin, quoted in Willison,* Reminiscences, *pp. 187-8.*

Benjamin Disraeli

116

*Saturday Night*

Sir John A. Macdonald, from an etching on copper by Harold Blackburn Harte, 1891.

Sir John and His Cabinet, 1886

# Sir John Takes a Look at Possible Successors

[His secretary, Sir Joseph Pope, recalled Sir John's opinion on the qualifications of his possible successors:]

Sir John Abbott: 'Why, he hasn't a single qualification for the office!'

Sir John Thompson: 'Thompson is very able and a fine fellow, but Ontario would never endure his turning Catholic.'

Sir Adolphe Caron: 'Caron is too much influenced by his hates – a fatal mistake in a public man, who should have no resentments.'

Sir Hector Langevin: 'There is no one else. . . . He has always been true to me.'

Mr. Mowat was here the other day and gave, of course, a pleasant dissertation. He is a most respectable man, and in any other position but the one he now holds [Premier of Ontario] would perform the duties of it most satisfactorily.

One strong point I admire about Mowat is his handwriting.

Lord Dufferin, one of the more learned governors general, and not a little proud of it, delivered an address in Greek at McGill University, at which Sir John and Sir Hector Langevin were present. A reporter subsequently described the occasion in the press with the comment: 'His Lordship spoke in the purest ancient Greek without mispronouncing a word or making the slightest grammatical solecism.'

'How did the reporter know that?' said Sir Hector to Sir John.

'I told him,' replied Sir John.

'But you don't know Greek.'

'True,' answered Sir John, 'but I know a little about politics.'

Sir John is by far the ablest public man in Canada. – *Earl of Dufferin.*

Sir John: 'The intention of the Government is, if it is the will of the House, to sit on Dominion Day.'

Hon. Edward Blake: 'Not on St. John's Day?'

Sir John: 'That is my day.'

Mr. Blake: 'No, the hon. gentleman is not yet canonized. It requires a long space of time, and a successful passing of the very serious ordeal of an inquisition, with the *advocatus diaboli* as chief accuser.'

Sir John: 'Will my hon. friend not take that office?'

119

# 'Old Tomorrow'

[Sir John, like most politicians, made far more promises than he could ever redeem. Delays in making appointments, and particularly where some advantage might lie in temporizing, were characteristic.

The nickname 'Old Tomorrow' was given late in Sir John's life. On February 5, 1885, the Hon. Edward Blake, Leader of the Opposition, asked from time to time when certain appointments were to be made. Sir John's reputation for delay in all such matters had long been recognized by both his opponents and his followers; and even those who failed to secure appointments were usually left with the feeling that they had been paid a compliment, for he had persuasive powers beyond the ordinary. With respect to the questions in the House that day, he used the expressions 'ere long' and 'tomorrow'. 'It is intended', he said, 'to fill the office of Minister of Railways ere long', and as he said it a voice (unidentified) called out 'tomorrow' and the House broke into a collective smile. Mr. Blake continued by asking when a Librarian of Parliament would be appointed.]

Sir John: 'A librarian has not yet been appointed; one will be appointed ere long – I was going to say "tomorrow" only I knew the honourable gentlemen would laugh.'

House of Commons Debates, *1885, Vol. I, p. 41*.

The term 'Old Tomorrow' was generally applied with kindly intent, and was accepted by Sir John with no apparent resentment. It is said that a friend, hearing that Sir John was to be given a peerage, asked him what title he would take. 'Lord Tomorrow,' he replied without a moment's hesitation.

[In at least one instance, long before the nickname was applied, it was to John A.'s advantage to suggest delay. In 1860, while Prime Minister of the old Province of Canada, he was twitted by the Opposition for a statement he had earlier made in reference to the choice of Ottawa as the new capital:]

Mr. Wilson: 'And the Attorney-General West said, speaking of the selection of Ottawa as the seat of government, "It was only done to humbug the French. I never intended to carry it out." '

John A. Macdonald: 'Where did I say that?'

Mr. Wilson: 'At the hustings in the Town of Kingston.'

Mr. McGee*: 'I have the affidavits in my desk, and can produce them at once if desired.'

John A. Macdonald: 'Oh, another day will answer just as well.'

[*D'Arcy McGee was at that period a Reformer, in opposition to Macdonald and the Conservatives.]

Photo by H. D. Topley, Public Archives of Canada

# The Youngest Graduate

[At the Convocation of the University of Toronto in June 1889 honorary degrees were conferred upon Sir John Macdonald, Oliver Mowat, and Edward Blake. The contemporary press noted Sir John's youthful appearance and attitude.]

Sir John, arrayed in the hood of an Oxford D.C.L., was the first to be summoned before the Vice-Chancellor, the sponsor being Sir Daniel Wilson. The Chieftain jumped up from his chair with almost youthful alacrity, smiled in his own characteristic way as he looked around him, and in fact bore himself through the short initiation with the feelings of a man proud of his position and surroundings. When the Vice-Chancellor [William Mulock] welcomed him as the youngest graduate so far, Sir John momentarily looked as if he enjoyed the novelty, and, as will be subsequently seen, he did not allow the opportunity to slip without an allusion which provoked laughter and delight all round.

Sir John, on turning round to the audience, was cheered to the echo. After the applause subsided he began by craving the indulgence of Convocation for not making a long speech. 'Pardon,' he said, 'my inexperience as the youngest graduate of this University.' (Laughter.) He was always interested in the University of Toronto, remembering that a son of his own is a brother graduate now. (Laughter.) It was his privilege to have had at one time something to do with the University of Toronto, claiming that he had led a successful fight in saving its endowment. There was a seductive proposition made to divide the endowment among the counties for grammar school purposes. He was conservative on this point, and was happy that as a member of the then Government he had the pleasure of signing the contract for the erection of the present building. In conclusion Sir John said that he sat at the cradle of the University, and now was proud to know the high position which it occupied as the foremost educational institution in the Province. (Applause.) Sir John then signed the register.

*Toronto* Globe, *June 8, 1889.*

Under the influence of Bishop Strachan the entrance of students to King's College, which inaugurated the University of Toronto, was restricted to those who would subscribe to a statement accepting the Thirty-Nine Articles, the basis of belief of the Church of England. But when Queen's University was being established in the 1840s, Macdonald used his influence to support entrance without religious tests of any kind.

Photo by Herbert Tilley, in James Hannay: *The Life and Times of Sir Leonard Tilley*

The Macdonalds and the Tilleys at Rivière du Loup, 1890
(Left to right) Lady Macdonald, Sir Leonard Tilley, Lady Tilley, Sir John Macdonald,
L. P. de W. Tilley; one of very few informal portraits of John A., who spent
many short holidays at Rivière du Loup.

# The Last Campaign

Before it had yet become dark the pretty central park, the Gore, famous all over the Dominion, was lighted up with innumerable and various coloured gas lamps. . . . Column after column of torchlighted forces wheeled into line from the neighbouring streets. Prancing horses and caravans of all descriptions bearing transparencies of political portent followed. . . . They marched and countermarched; they played and they tooted their horns; they cheered and they shouted . . . fireworks were started . . . it could be seen at a glance that the finest political procession ever organized in this country was under way. As far as the eye could reach, the darkness of night was pierced by the light of myriads of torches, and an incessant discharge of Roman candles and rockets illuminated the line of march. Ten bands . . . numerous transparencies bearing appropriate mottoes . . . almost all the seats [in the Palace Rink in Hamilton] had been reserved for the ladies. . . . When Sir John entered there was an outburst of enthusiasm . . . the ladies stood up and waved handkerchiefs and cheered with all the power of their voices . . . the back of the platform was covered with an immense Union Jack. . . .

A portion of the Drill Hall, where the meeting was held, was apportioned to the ladies, no gentlemen allowed in. In the rest of the hall the general public could fight it out for breathing room. Seats had been provided for 4,800. . . . When Sir John rose to speak a large Union Jack, about three feet long by two feet wide, made of flowers, the same on both sides, attached to a staff about six feet high covered with smilax, was presented to him – a gift from the 'loyal Conservative ladies of London'. . . . The ladies attended in force, all armed with small flags which they waved like crazy children until the excitement was so great that many of them stood upon their chairs and joined in the cheering of the crowd behind them.

*Macpherson,* Life of Macdonald, *II, pp. 410-13.*

R. R. Osgoode, from a painting in the Ontario Parliament Buildings

'Old Union Jack'
Sir John addressing a night gathering during his last campaign.

# We Look to England

I think you will agree with me that there is somewhere and among some people a conspiracy to drive Canada into the arms of the United States to be as obstructive as possible and as annoying as possible to this country. . . . We have no such questions as the Negro question, which is looming up so disastrously in the United States; we have no large nuclei of foreign anarchists; you saw what they did at Chicago a while ago. We have no such thing as elected judges, where the people elect men who will decide according to the wishes of the majority. We look up to England and to English tradition for our guidance; we have everything to lose – much more than money's worth – we have everything to lose in being severed from England; we have everything to gain by the benign influence of Her Majesty's Government, a free queen over a free people, but governed by principles of religion, by principles of equality, and by principles of morality which a democracy never had and never will have.* (Applause.) . . . But if it should happen that we should be absorbed in the United States the name of Canada would be literally forgotten; we should have the State of Ontario, State of Quebec, and State of Nova Scotia, and State of New Brunswick; every one of the provinces would be a state; but where is the grand, the glorious name of Canada? . . . All I can say is that not with me, or not by the action of my friends, or not by the action of the people of Canada, will such a disaster come upon us. I believe that this election, which is a great crisis, and upon which so much depends, will show to the Americans that we prize our country as much as they do, that we would fight for our existence as much as they fought for the preservation of their independence. (Hear, hear.) That the spirit of our fathers, which fought and won battle after battle, still exists in our sons; and if I thought it was otherwise I would say the sooner the grass was growing over my grave the better, rather than that I should see the degradation of the country which I have loved so much and which I have served so long. (Loud and prolonged applause.)

*Toronto* Empire, *February 18, 1891.*

---

*This derogatory reference to democracy, often equated with mob rule, was characteristic of the times. In Sir John's day it was Conservative policy to restrict voting to property owners, 'with a stake in the country'.

Sir John was very proud of this mink-lined coat given him by his supporters.

Public Archives of Canada

# Aux Electeurs du Canada, 1891

La question que vous serez bientôt appelés à résoudre se réduit à ceci : risquerons-nous de perdre le riche héritage que nous ont laissé nos ancêtres et nous soumettrons-nous à la taxe directe, pour le soi-disant privilège de voir notre tarif fait à Washington, avec la perspective de devenir, en dernier ressort, portion de l'union américaine?

Je recommande des questions au jugement de tout le peuple canadien, avec la pleine confiance que vous proclamerez au monde entier votre détermination de vous montrer dignes de la distinction flatteuse dont vous jouissez : d'être du nombre des plus loyaux sujets de notre bien aimée Souveraine.

Pour ce qui me concerne, ma conduite est toute tracée : Je suis né sujet anglais, et sujet anglais je mourrai. De toutes mes forces et jusqu'à mon dernier soupir, je m'opposerai à cette trahison voilée qui tend, au moyen d'appâts sordides et mercenaires, à détourner le peuple de son allégeance. Pendant tout le cours de ma carrière politique qui date de près d'un demi-siècle, j'ai été fidèle à mon pays et à ses plus chers intérêts et c'est avec une égale confiance que je fais appel aux hommes qui m'ont honoré de leur appui dans le passé, et à la jeunesse d'aujourd'hui, l'espoir de la patrie, la gardienne de ses destinées dans l'avenir, pour qu'ils me prêtent leur aide commune, en ce dernier effort de ma vie, afin d'assurer l'unité de l'empire et la perpétuité de notre liberté politique et commerciale.

Je demeure, Messieurs,

Votre fidèle serviteur,

John A. Macdonald.

Ottawa, 7 février 1891.

[Sir John did not speak French, but could read it with reasonable facility. In his addresses he frequently used French phrases.]

128

# Facsimile of the Original Draft of Sir John's Last Address

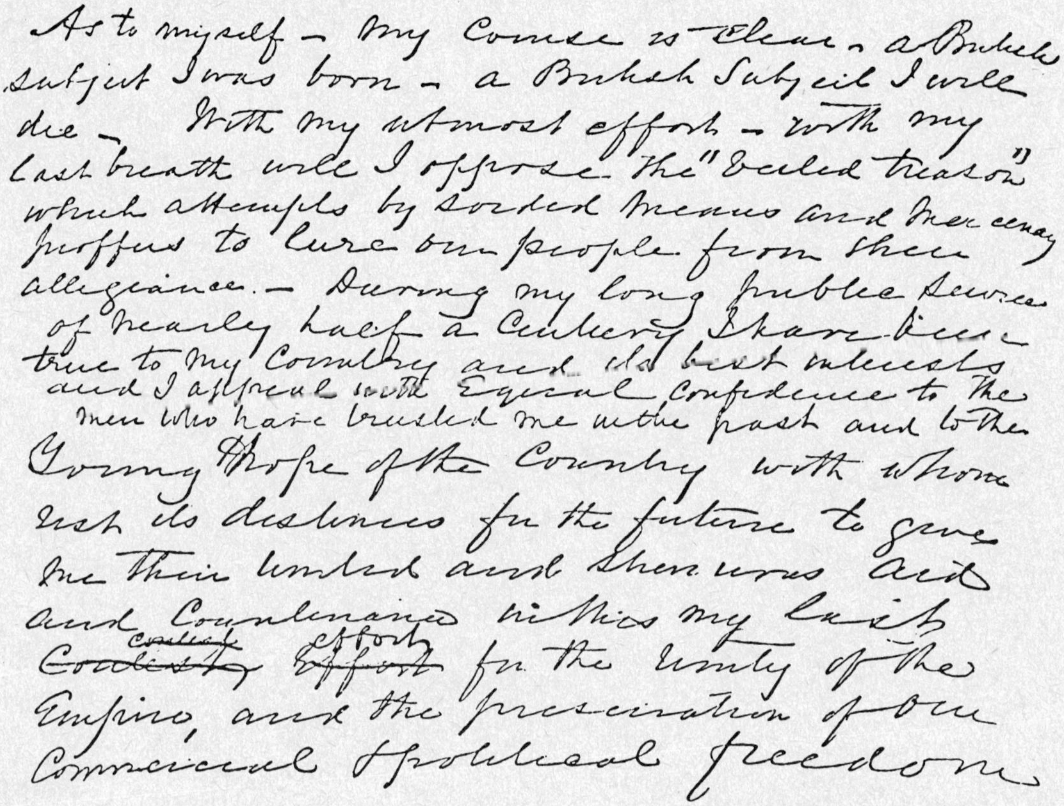

As to myself – My Course is Clear – a British subject I was born – a British Subject I will die – With my utmost effort – with my last breath will I oppose the "Veiled treason" which attempts by sordid means and mercenary proffers to lure our people from their allegiance. – During my long public service of nearly half a Century I have been true to my Country and its best interests and I appeal with Equal Confidence to the men who have trusted me in the past and to the Young Hope of the Country with whom rest its destinies for the future to give me their united and their warm Aid and Countenance in this my last ~~Contest~~ ~~effort~~ for the Unity of the Empire, and the preservation of our Commercial & political freedom

Public Archives of Canada

130

J. W. Bengough, Rapid Grip and Batten Ltd.

'I'll rant as well as thou!' – Shakespeare

# Sir John's Last Birthday Mail, 1891

Sir John Macdonald always observed his birthday, and liked others to remember it. On the 11th of January the mail bag was of portentous size, while all day the telegraph brought congratulations from far and wide. Among many congratulatory letters he received was one from an unknown little maiden, who wrote him a childish note to announce that her birthday was on the same day as his. . . . She thought it proper, however, to remind him that a certain nice boy named Charles was coming to her birthday party, if her mother would permit, and also that long long ago she had written to a boy who had not answered her. This she thought was very mean. Adding 'If you get this letter do not forget to write if you git it'. To the letter Sir John replied:

Earnscliffe, Ottawa, January 6, 1891.
My dear little Friend,

I am glad to get your letter, and to know that next Sunday you and I will be of the same age. I hope and believe, however, that you will see many more birthdays than I shall, and I trust that every birthday may find you strong in health, and prosperous, and happy.

I think it was mean of that young fellow not to answer your letter. You see, I have been longer in the world than he, and know more than he does of what is due to young ladies.

I send you a dollar note, with which pray buy some small keepsake to remember me by, and,

Believe me yours sincerely,
John A. Macdonald.

*Sir Joseph Pope,* Memoirs of the Right Honourable Sir John Alexander Macdonald *(Ottawa, 1894),* p. 645.

SIR JOHN SPEAKS.

*The Dominion Illustrated*

# Sir John's Last Day in the House, May 22, 1891

[On May 22, 1891, there was considerable discussion in the House of Commons relative to the participation of Sir Charles Tupper in the recent election, for his position was High Commissioner in England. Sir John himself could participate but little because of ill health during the campaign. Tupper spoke for Sir John at Kingston, as well as elsewhere in the province. Particularly persistent was William Paterson, the member for Brant, but Sir Richard Cartwright and others participated, asking why Tupper had left his duties in England to electioneer in Ontario, and at whose expense.]

Mr. Paterson: 'Might I ask the First Minister, did the High Commissioner tell the truth to the people of Kingston? . . .'

Sir John: 'Well, Mr. Chairman, I cannot resist the seductive tones of my hon. friend and I may answer him: Sir Charles Tupper did go there at my request and he made the speech at my instance, and I fancy that his speech must have had a considerable influence, because in the previous election I was elected by a majority of seventeen, and after Sir Charles Tupper made this speech I was elected by a majority that only wanted seventeen of 500. You see I was pretty wise in asking Sir Charles to go there and make a speech for me.'

Mr. Paterson: 'You would be wise if you stopped him at that point.'

Sir John: 'I will go a little further, and I will say that Sir Charles Tupper came out from England to give us the advantage of his skill, and influence, and eloquence, at my special request.'

[Questioned subsequently as to Tupper's lack of influence when he spoke elsewhere, whether Sir John had lost his shrewdness, or Sir Charles his eloquence:]

Sir John: 'I will tell you what he did: he lost his voice.'

[A little later Mr. Paterson pursued the matter of the costs of Tupper's trip:]

Sir John: 'I am not aware that any of the High Commissioner's expenses were paid out of the public service, but I will enquire.'

Mr. Paterson: 'I suppose his trips from England to this country and back again find a place in the expenses?'

Sir John: 'That may be, but I cannot say.'

[Following another question as to why Tupper was recalled to Canada, he said:] 'I have already stated what I asked him to come out for.' Then, when Sir Richard Cartwright asked about subsidies given roads and railways in Kingston, Sir John said, 'You did not do much for them.'

[These were his last words in the House of Commons. Sir John moved much more than usual about the House that evening among the members, and in the light of his succeeding illness it was a memorable occasion. He left the House with Sir Mackenzie Bowell, and when they parted he said, 'It is late, Bowell. Good-night.']

House of Commons Debates, *1891, III, pp. 426-41.*

The Funeral Procession Moving from the
Senate Chamber

# The Nation Mourning a Nation's Hero

The great chieftain of the Conservative Party has gone the way of all flesh, and although he is succeeded he can have no successor. The face and form which for many years enlivened these pages have departed for ever. It is a satisfaction to feel, as we do, that although few numbers of *Grip* have appeared without 'John A.' being depicted in some shape, we have never treated him with less than justice. This he was not slow to admit himself on the occasion of the only interview we ever had with him, and which took place at Ottawa a few years ago. '*Grip* has been conducted most fairly and impartially so far,' said he. 'I hope you will never let it get into the control of either party.' It was not the least of Sir John's gifts as a public man (from *Grip's* standpoint) that he had a face supremely good for caricature purposes. In that respect, as well as in others, we may say with Hamlet, 'We ne'er shall look upon his like again.' This journal, however, like Her Majesty's Government, must be carried on. May he rest in peace.

Grip, *June 13, 1891.*

June Eighth [1891]. – On entering the vestibule of the St. Lawrence Hall [Montreal] this morning, it was at once apparent that something serious was agitating the public mind. One name was on every person's lip, only to be spoken in whispers and with reverence. The common conversation was not of stocks or shares, of buying or selling, but of the demise of Canada's noblest son, her most distinguished citizen. The empire was weeping its departed statesman; the nation mourning a nation's hero. Sir John Macdonald was dead; the 'Father of his country', as he was now designated. In driving about the city I saw everywhere signs of mourning and sorrow. Scores of Canadian Ensigns were fluttering, half-mast high, upon the ships in the harbour, and upon the Parliament and most of the other public buildings, whilst mourning emblems were noticeable in every direction; and the sole topic of conversation was about the great and irreparable loss the country had sustained. The difference of political opinion, that must ever exist where representative government is established, was forgotten for the time, and Conservative and Liberal alike were ready to say something good of the great statesman who had been removed.

*William Smith,* A Yorkshireman's Trip to the United States and Canada *(1892), p. 278.*

The Body of Sir John A. Macdonald Lying in State in the Senate Chamber, Ottawa

*The Dominion Illustrated*

137

# 'J. W. Bengough's Tribute To Sir John'

BORN AT GLASGOW, JAN. 11, 1815;
DIED AT OTTAWA, JUNE 6, 1891.

\*    \*    \*

Dead! Dead! And now before
The threshold of bereaved Earnscliffe stand
In spirit, all who dwell within our land
From shore to shore!

Before that black-draped gate,
Men, women, children mourn the Premier gone,
For many loved and worshipped old Sir John,
And none could hate.

And he is dead they say!
The words confuse and mock the general ear –
What! can there yet be House and Members
here
And no John A.?

So long he lived and reigned
Like merry monarch of some olden line,
Whose subjects questioned not his right divine
But just obeyed

His will's e'en faintest breath,
We had forgotten – 'midst affairs of State,
'Midst Hansard, Second Readings, and Debate,
Such things as Death!

Swift came the dread eclipse
Of faculty, and limb and life at last,
Ere to the Judge of all the earth he passed
With silent lips,

But not insensate heart!
He was no harsh self-righteous Pharisee –
The tender Christ compassioned such as he,
And took their part.

As to his Statesman-fame,
Let History calm his wondrous record read,
And write the Truth, and give him honest meed
Of praise or blame.

J. W. B.

Grip, *June 13, 1891.*

'The Empty Saddle'
J. W. Bengough, Rapid Grip and Batten Ltd.

# Rt. Hon. Sir JOHN MACDONALD
## K. C. B., PREMIER

Died at
Ottawa, Saturday, June 6, 1891
Interment at
Cataraqui Cemetery, Kingston
Thursday, June 11

## FUNERAL ARRANGEMENTS

The Funeral Cortege will leave the City Hall, Kingston, at 2 p.m.

All societies and delegations from public lodges must take their places in line by 1.30 p.m.

ROUTE:—Direct from City Hall along Ontario Street to Princess Street, and direct to Cataraqui Cemetery

## THE ORDER OF FUNERAL

Kingston Firemen
Masonic Order
Gananoque Carriage Works Band
Canton Kingston I.O.O.F.

Cataraqui & Kingston Lodges, I.O.O.F.
Manchester Order Oddfellows
'Prentice Boys
Orange Brethren
Orange Young Britons
Orange True Blues
Independent Order Foresters
Canadian Order Foresters
Ancient Order Foresters
Catholic Order Foresters

St. Patrick's Society
C. M. Ben. Ass'n
Y. I. C. Ben. Ass'n
A. O. United Workmen
Select Knights
Royal Arcanum
St. Andrew's Society
Sons of Scotland
Sons of England
St. George's Society

ALL ABOVE TO WALK 4 ABREAST

Kingston Police
4th Regiment Cavalry, 8 abreast
Bands of Battery A and 14th P. W. O. Rifles
Clergy
Funeral Director
Flowers
Pallbearers    Hoarse    Pallbearers
Mourners
Governor-General and Staff
Col. Gzowski representing Her Majesty the Queen
Her Majesty's Troops and Naval Officers
Lt.-Governors of Provinces and Staffs
Archbishops and Bishops
Members of Cabinet
Speaker of Senate
Chief Judges of Courts of Law and Equity
Members of Senate
Speaker House of Commons
Puisne Judges of Courts of Law and Equity
Members House of Commons
Members Executive Councils of Provinces
Speakers of Legislative Councils and Members
Speakers of Legislative Assembly and Members
Consuls of Foreign Powers
Deputy Ministers
Law Societies
Officers of Militia
Mayor and Corporation of Kingston
Deputations from Cities and Towns
Citizens
Carriages

W. M. DRENNAN, Funeral Director

G. M. Adam, *Canada's Patriot Statesman*

The Funeral Procession, Princess Street, Kingston

# Lady Macdonald's Reply to Conservative Caucus Address, 1891

Ottawa, June 18. – Enthusiasm pervaded the Conservative caucus room this morning, and the cheering inside exuded through the closed doors, and found its way up and down the corridors. The occasion was the first meeting of the party under its new leadership. The attendance was very full, and there were present the Conservative Senators as well as the Conservative Commoners. At the commencement of the proceedings the following letter addressed to the chairman was read from Lady Macdonald in reply to the address of condolence which had been sent to her:

LETTER FROM LADY MACDONALD
Earnscliffe, Ottawa, June 17, 1891.

I have received and read with a proud satisfaction the address you forwarded to me from the Conservative members of both Houses of Parliament, conveying, in words that are each one a comfort and consolation to me, their sense of my loss and their own. Will you do me the favour to say to these gentlemen, my husband's true and devoted friends, with what a swelling heart I dwell on their loving testimony to the greatness of him, whose useful, kindly, Christian life it will ever be our high privilege to remember. I thank these dear friends with tears, not of sorrow, for such a life and such a death are beyond the reach of common sorrow, but with tears of gratitude and affection, in acknowledgment of their love for him and faithfulness to him through many years and many battles. Will you tell them from me at some time, where all can hear, that I, his widow and broken-hearted in my loneliness and desolation, venture to ask from them a last and lasting tribute to my husband's dear memory. I ask that that tribute shall be a firm and united support of the policy and principles our great leader lived and died to maintain and carry out. I appeal to them with all the power my words can convey to do now and in the future what they and I know would be my husband's wish and desire, could those lips, silent on earth forevermore, speak on this or any other crisis of our country's history – to stand side by side, shoulder to shoulder, regardless of irritation, self-interest, or seeming reverse, with no goal but Canada's success; to follow, in short, the splendid example left to us, and to carry out, with no sign of division or faltering, the plans and purposes that lay so near Sir John's heart. I shall watch, so long as my life lasts, with earnest anxiety the progress of public affairs, as for the last twenty years I have been proud to do; and pray, as I have always prayed, that the Almighty Ruler of all men would of His mercy grant wisdom, foresight, and firmness to the policy and councils of the great Conservative party.

Believe me, your sincere friend,

(Signed)                    Agnes Macdonald.

*Newspaper clipping of June 1891, J. Alex. Edmison Collection.*

Henry Sandham, Public Archives of Canada

This portrait, described by Lady Macdonald as 'the most speaking likeness of Sir John',
hangs in the Centre Block of the Parliament Buildings, Ottawa.

# Criticism and Praise

[The most bitter commentator on Sir John Macdonald among contemporary politicians was Sir Richard Cartwright (Lennox and Addington), long an 'independent Conservative' but latterly a Liberal with a particular animosity for John A. In one of his less hostile moods he gave this estimate of the reasons for Macdonald's success as a leader:]

Largely to his personality. He was 'John A.', and there was no other like him. But he was an excellent parliamentarian and indefatigable in the work of keeping his party together. He might and did neglect his departmental work, but he never neglected his *rôle* as leader of his party. He had an immense correspondence, which he preserved with jealous care, and could generally lay his hand on any document he wanted, even after a long lapse of years. I should say that in Ontario there was scarcely a single riding in which Sir John could not count a score or more of men occupying more or less influential positions, every one of whom either owed their appointment to him, or had been under obligations to him of one sort or the other, or of whom he knew something they would not care to have made public. In this way he could generally always obtain a pretty good idea of the political situation in any quarter, and very often mould public opinion pretty much as he desired. This, perhaps, was an incident due to his very long political career, but he understood thoroughly how to make the most of it. *Per contra*, he was thoroughly unscrupulous in making any statements to gain a point, and very jealous, sometimes absurdly so, of any man whom he thought might prove a possible competitor for the leadership. . . . I will only add that Sir John was always anxious, as far as political exigencies would permit, to maintain the dignity of the Bench, and also that if he exacted great sacrifices in a pecuniary way from many of his followers he made great sacrifices himself. . . .

As for myself, my relations with him for many years had been so strained that I have some hesitation in expressing my opinion of his career. He had many good points* and not a few of the qualities which go to make a public man a popular idol, as indeed he had become and in a sense continues to be to this day, but he did incalculable mischief to Canada, and . . . grievously degraded the whole tone of public life and political morality in Canada.

*Sir Richard Cartwright*, Reminiscences *(Toronto, 1912), pp. 48 and 302.*

---

*'I will say this for that old scoundrel John A. Macdonald', Cartwright once said, 'that if he once gave you his word, you could rely upon it.'

Sir John had a wonderful influence over many men. They would go through fire and water to serve him, did serve him, and got, some of them, little or no reward. But they served him because they loved him, and because with all his great powers they saw in him their own frailties. He abounded in the right kind of charity. And speaking of the love his friends and followers had for him, Mr. Pope dwells on the 'old guard' and the old loyalty to the chief. So it was, but there were dark days also, when even those who afterwards enrolled themselves in the guard passed by on the other side. If ever there was a man in low water it was Sir John as I saw him one day in the winter of 1875, coming out of the House in the bitter air, dressed in a Red River sash and cap, tottering down the hill to the eastern gateway alone, others passing him with a wide sweep. The lesson of Sir John's life is that he pulled himself out of those days and trials into higher and more solid footing. But Sir John's real 'old guard' were not the men who stood with him at Ottawa, but the greater old guard who stood and fought for him in every township year after year, and to whom a call by name or a nod of the head was all the recompense they got and yet the recompense they most prized. Sir John has been praised for his statesmanship, and for this too I give him all praise. But his statesmanship was limited to two things: carrying on the Government when no one else could do it – and do it so well and so continuously – and forging the country together. He originated no great principle. He appropriated, however, freely from others when an opportunity offered, or when he thought another's idea would lead to or keep him in office.

*W. F. Maclean,* Canadian Magazine.

Sir John Macdonald was rarely at fault in those whom he trusted. . . . Human as he was, he was not too susceptible to flattery. Not by adulation did men obtain his confidence and recognition. . . . He wanted to govern with material that was workable, and his supreme objects were to unify Canada and maintain the connection with the Empire. . . . He was sensitive to the predilections of Quebec not only because he needed the support of the French Province, but because he believed that Quebec should have co-ordinate authority in the Confederation and that unity of feeling was the essential condition of national stability.

Sir John Macdonald was not a reformer, but he was more than an opportunist. He was reluctant to unsettle public opinion by revolutionary proposals; . . . he seldom lost confidence in his own genius to govern. . . . But the substantial consistency of Sir John Macdonald's career is good evidence that he directed while he managed, and that he abandoned none of his essential convictions for office. It is true that he adopted Protection with reluctance. As he said himself, 'It's devilish hard for a free trader to make a Protectionist speech.' . . . If he moved slowly it was because he hesitated to break new ground, and because he was very unwilling to be misunderstood in Great Britain. . . .

He sanctioned bribery and misuse of public appropriations for party purposes. But in the party by which he was opposed there was a considerable admixture of pretence and hypocrisy. George Brown was as unscrupulous in elections as Sir John Macdonald. Mackenzie and Blake set their faces against corruption and to a degree they prevailed. But no one who has knowledge believes that corruption ended when the Conservative party, twenty-three years ago, entered upon its long service in Opposition. . . . Other Canadian statesmen had great qualities which were not his in equal degree, and freedom from faults which he possessed, but in the sum of his service and in high fitness for the tasks of his time he was greater than any of his contemporaries. I recall that May day when Sir Hector Langevin arose in Parliament and read in halting sentences and with deep emotion the bulletin from Earnscliffe which gave the first certain intelligence of his mortal illness. Men flocked down from right and left to the centre of the Chamber, affected by an instant common grief, lifted in a moment above all rancour and contention, and no one who looked into their faces or caught their hushed voices could say from what he saw or heard who was Conservative or Liberal. . . . I think of the gloom which lay over the country until the end came, and the universal sorrow which bound all Canadians together on June 6th, 1891, when he passed out of the turmoil of the world into whatsoever God willed for him. It was no common man who so touched a nation's heart, and as time passes we see his stature more clearly and forget the way in which some things were done in gratitude for all that was achieved.

*Willison,* Reminiscences, *pp. 197-200.*

# His Ability to Lead and to Inspire Men

The fiftieth anniversary of the death of Sir John A. Macdonald has seemed to my colleagues and myself an occasion on which a national tribute should be paid to the memory of one whose name and achievements have become an imperishable part of the heritage of Canada.

A formidable opponent and, later, an honoured colleague of Sir John Macdonald, Joseph Howe of Nova Scotia, reminded his day and generation that 'a wise nation preserves its records, gathers up its muniments, decorates the tombs of its illustrious dead, repairs its great public structures, and fosters national pride and love of country by perpetual references to the sacrifices and glories of the past'.

It is in the spirit so eloquently expressed in these words that we, of another generation, old and young, from near and far, of different religious and political faiths, welcome this opportunity to commemorate the life and work of the first Prime Minister of Canada. We are proud to be assembled today in the city with which his great career was so intimately associated, and to surround, on this anniversary, the monument which citizens of Kingston have erected to his memory. When this brief service is concluded, the wreaths we place on the tomb of the illustrious dead will be an expression, as he would have wished, of our common patriotism. . . .

Sir Wilfrid Laurier, in the tribute he paid Sir John Macdonald at the time of his death, said of Sir John that he was endowed with those inner, subtle graces of the soul which win and keep the hearts of men. Sir Wilfrid had, I think, in mind Sir John's loyalty to country, to cause, and to friends; his tact, his kindness, his resourcefulness; his humour, his long youthfulness of heart – most of all, perhaps, the genuine love he had for his fellow men. Those qualities begot in him an outlook on life which was at once tolerant and generous. Combined with vision which came with youth, and wisdom, which ripened with the years, they gave to him his ability to lead and to inspire men.

*Rt. Hon. W. L. Mackenzie King at Commemoration Service, Kingston, June 7, 1941.*

Statue of Sir John Macdonald, Ottawa
Unveiled on Dominion Day, 1895.
Public Archives of Canada

## DATE DUE

| | | | |
|---|---|---|---|
| Mar 13 | | | |
| Apr 12 | | | |
| Apr 19 | | | |
| May 3. | | | |
| Jun 5. | | | |
| Hensall | | | |
| Aug 11 | | | |
| | | | |
| | | | |
| | | | |
| | | | |
| | | | |
| | | | |
| | | | |
| | | | |
| | | | |

CAT. NO. 1137